THE FRAIL OCEAN

THE FRAIL OCEAN

*A Blueprint for Change
in the 1990s and Beyond*

UPDATED EDITION

by
Wesley Marx

CHESTER, CONNECTICUT

The following photographs appear courtesy of both Tom Stack & Associates and the individual photographers whose names accompany the photo descriptions: kelp forest, Dave B. Fleetham; Glen Canyon Dam, Rich Buzzelli; South Padre Island, Matt Bradley; coastal storm, Hal Clason; fishing boat, Byron Augustin; Aruba shoreline, Jack Swenson; oil spill, Ken W. Davis; industrial pollution, Gary Milburn. Remaining photographs are by the author.

Portions of this book were published previously in *The Atlantic Monthly*, *Reader's Digest*, *Coast & Ocean*, and *Landscape Architecture*.

Library of Congress Cataloging-in-Publication Data

Marx, Wesley.
    The frail ocean : a blueprint for change in the 1990s and beyond / by Wesley Marx. —Updated ed.
        p.   cm.
    ISBN 0-87106-542-8
    1. Marine resources conservation.   I. Title.
GC1018.M313   1991
333.91'64—dc20
                                        91-13674
                                        CIP

Manufactured in the United States of America
First Globe Pequot Edition/First Printing

*To Judy, Chris,
Heather, and Ty*

Table of Contents

PART FOUR: THE TOLL OF POLLUTION

Photographs follow page 98.

Foreword

M odern ecological thinking is just now beginning to focus
on the importance of our oceans to the well-being of the
world's environment. Pictures from space remind us dramatically that seven-tenths of our planet is ocean. Science has determined that our oceans act as the lungs of the planet,
supplying us with the majority of Earth's oxygen. Technology,
reaching out to explore the solar system, has revealed that Earth
alone has oceans.

We are, however, also learning that for the first time in
history the vitality of our oceans is in jeopardy. The thinning of
the Earth's ozone layer threatens both the source of the oceans'
food web and their capacity to cool the planet. As the result of
75 percent of us having moved to within fifty miles of one of our
coastlines, sixteen trillion gallons of sewage and industrial waste
are dumped yearly into coastal waters. Shellfishing beds are
routinely closed or restricted. Overfishing threatens to make our
oceans aquatic deserts. Pollution and coastal development are
killing marine mammals, including endangered species.

Wes Marx's book *The Frail Ocean* is an important contribution to our new and troubled awareness of oceans. In accessible terms, it explains the diverse nature of our oceans and the problems they face. The book also details solutions to the problems.

We in the environmental movement have proposed a plan to save America's and the world's oceans. Stop all forms of ocean dumping, including sewage and radioactive waste. Reduce and eliminate from the waste stream all toxins that routinely find their way to the ocean. Impose stiff sanctions and civil fines for illegal dumping. Ratify international treaties that would not only eliminate ozone-depleting gases from the atmosphere but also protect marine mammals and sustain world fisheries. Establish permanent marine sanctuaries to preserve the oceans from industrial development.

The value of *The Frail Ocean* is that it supports and explains this plan in such a way as to allow the lay person to embrace it, live by it, and fight for it. Indeed, if we are concerned enough to follow this plan, we can save our seas. Only if we do, though, will we continue our odyssey on this, the Water Planet.

ROBERT H. SULNICK
executive director,
American Oceans Campaign

Introduction

José Rosario reminded his lifeguards to wear the latest in beach accessories: plastic gloves to pick up another batch of washed-up hypodermic needles and shoes to avoid being punctured by this recent addition to beach ecology. There would be plenty of time to look for needles. The Staten Island section of the Gateway National Seashore was closed again to the New York–New Jersey public it was supposed to serve. The reason this time: a sewer plant overflow. A week before, it was washed-up garbage. Next week, it might be polluted storm runoff. Park Superintendent Rosario looked out toward the sun-splashed Atlantic Ocean and noted, "Sometimes I think there is more garbage than water out there."

Downcoast, a motel owner received another phone cancellation for a vacation reservation. "This pollution is worse than a hurricane. A hurricane is over in a day. Who knows when this pollution will end?" asked William Meis.

Residents and hotel operators along the North Sea, around the Mediterranean Basin, and throughout much of the global shore were also wondering about the answer to this question. In

1989 and 1990, massive oil spills competed with sewage spills in closing down more sections of our coastline. In 1991, a new style of oil spill debuted on the world scene. A desperate Iraq was accused of deliberately leaking oil into the Persian Gulf to harass its foes in the Middle East conflict. The resulting spill—the world's largest to date—threatened to make the Gulf itself a prime casualty of the war. Never before have we been so skilled in the marine arts, from surfboarding to submarining, and never before have the global shore and our oceans been so burdened by such a hideous hodgepodge of our liquid and solid castaways.

It may be difficult to accept the fact that our progress can defile the ocean. The ocean has long been considered an impenetrable redoubt of nature. We celebrate its omnipotence in verse, in music, and in art. George Gordon Byron, Lord Byron, who loved to bodysurf in the North Sea, wrote of the joys of the "society where none intrudes" and wondered at its power:

> Roll on, thou deep and dark blue ocean—roll!
> Ten thousand fleets sweep over thee in vain;
> Man marks the earth with ruin—his control
> Stops with the shore.

The ocean stirred Melville, Conrad, Stevenson, and many other of our most distinguished writers to their finest achievements. An ocean marsh was enough to inspire Sidney Lanier:

> Oh, what is aboard in the marsh and the
>   terminal sea?
> Somehow my soul seems suddenly free
> From the weighing of fate and the sad
>   discussion of sin.

Musicians and artists have been inspired, too. Claude Debussy's best-known work is a hymn to the sea. Winslow Homer, a fledgling artist in search of a subject, began painting the ocean off the New Jersey shore. Then he moved north, set up a portable painting booth on the surf-dashed cliffs of Maine, and donned oilskins to paint during savage storms. For the last twenty-seven years of his life, Homer, a semirecluse, painted the sea in all its moods. Today, his work is admired in museums throughout the world.

No other natural phenomenon on this planet—not even mountains five miles high, rivers spilling over cliffs, or redwood forests—evokes such reverence. Yet this same "all-powerful" ocean now proves as slavishly subservient to natural laws as a moth caught by candlelight or a rose seed blown into the Atlantic. The ocean obeys. It heeds. It complies. It has its tolerances and its stresses. When these are exceeded, the ocean falters. Fish stocks can be depleted. The nurseries of marine life can be buried. Beaches can erode. The sea itself can host substances that when taken up by oysters and clams can poison us. We have become a demanding taskmaster in the marine environment, but our shores and seas are endowed with limits that cannot always tolerate our ambitions or errors.

For more than two decades, scientists and environmental groups have warned that we are losing our natural marine heritage. Steps have been taken to clean up our marine act. In the United States, the public has been willing to fund billions of dollars worth of better sewage treatment. In some cases, we have learned how to restore degraded wetlands and mangrove forests. Impressive-sounding legislation has been passed: the Marine Mammal Protection Act, the Clean Water Act, the Fishery Conservation and Development Act. At the international level, a lengthy United Nations–sponsored Law of the Sea Conference culminated in a Law of the Sea Convention that was hailed as a "Magna Charta for the Seas."

Why can this legislative armada seem so defenseless against blood-test needles on the beach, pathogens in clams, and shorelines with too much plastic debris and not enough sand grains? Time and again, we tend to overestimate the ocean as a cornucopia of resources that will prolong our affluence and bootstrap developing nations into prosperity. At the same time, we tend to underestimate its need for careful understanding and use. The condition of our shores and seas is posing very painful questions about our traditional way of doing things, including our ability to govern ourselves on a watery planet. Clearly, the oceans will play a critical role as we act out our ultimate fate on this planet. Yet our attitudes toward the sea can be shot through with contradictions and conflicts, mistaken expectations and overlooked opportunities. We have just begun to learn the real meaning of living on a watery planet.

To explore the marine challenge, this book is divided into four sections. The first section explores the challenge of wisely managing our living marine resources, from sea forests of kelp to pods of whales. The second section explores how critical marine processes transcend national boundaries and require global as well as national responses. The third section explores how our actions on land can alter, if not destroy, coastal landforms critical to a safe and productive marine future. The fourth section explores how we use the marine environment as an all-purpose dump—sometimes by accident, more often by intention—for our spiraling wasteloads and how we can rise above this damaging practice. The concluding chapter explores how we have an opportunity to reverse, not just slow down, the degradation of our shores and seas. For too long, the fate of the marine environment has been subordinate to policy decisions regarding federal farm subsidies, packaging design, inland dam projects, timber cuts, and real estate needs. Now is the time to place the fate of our shores and seas in the forefront of public policy.

PART ONE

Managing Our Marine Resources

CHAPTER ONE

Seaweed: The Ocean's Unsung Gift

M emorials to women or to foreigners are rare in Japan. Yet overlooking Ariake Bay in southern Japan is a bronze plaque of Dr. Kathleen Drew Baker of Great Britain. How did she earn this unique honor? By her research on a modest plant we have usually dismissed as "seaweed."

Today, in a world running short of conventional food and energy resources, lowly seaweed is emerging as a dark horse candidate. It is almost as if the crabgrass that bedevils our lawns had suddenly become a cash crop. At the same time, we are learning that seaweed, like our forests on land, must be carefully managed.

This is heady status for a plant that bears no flowers or fruit, exudes no sweet scents, and inspires few songwriters and poets. Lying in mounds on a summer beach, ringed by buzzing flies, seaweed does indeed seem uninspiring. But would we judge a redwood tree on the basis of one branch adrift at sea?

My own attitude toward seaweed changed abruptly while I was learning to scuba dive off southern California. Friends encouraged me to dive into underwater "forests" of kelp, a large, brownish seaweed. Forests at sea? Show me.

The plants that lay shriveled on the beach unfurled into lanky, vinelike "fronds" that swayed in unison with passing swells. The silent motion seemed menacing, a danse macabre ready to embrace an intruder. But the eerie mood gradually ebbed. Underwater, the sprawling kelp that formed a dense canopy on the surface divided into arborlike columns. The kelp's brown cast, which looked so dull on the beach, glowed golden under the sunbeams that filtered through the canopy. No rustling forest in autumn color could rival this submarine radiance.

I hovered in the water, like a hawk in a summer updraft. Schools of fish passed like rain showers. A seal torpedoed toward me, then veered away in a flashy somersault. A pelican dropped from the sky in a cascade of silvery bubbles to gulp a billful of smelt. Ever since that day, I have preferred my forests underwater, where I needn't worry about blisters on my feet. And between "hikes" in the kelp forests, I have tried to learn more about kelp and other seaweeds—"marine algae," scientists call them—of the world's oceans.

While their structure appears similar to that of land plants, marine algae lack true stems, roots, and leaves. A rootlike holdfast anchors the plant to the seabed. Leaflike "blades" dangle from the stemlike "stipe." Many algae are dainty, lacy plants that glisten like living jewels in tide pools. Their nicknames—mermaid's hair, pearly moss, sweet tangle, feather boa, fairy's butter—reflect this beauty.

The plant that forms my beloved submarine forests is called giant kelp. It is the largest seaweed, weighing up to 300 pounds and able to grow more than a hundred feet long. Gas-filled bulbs at the base of each blade help buoy up the massive plants. (As a child, I cast the dried bulbs into camp fires, where they resounded like organic firecrackers.) Giant kelp's fronds can streak toward the sunlit surface at a rate of two feet a day. No other plant can grow so rapidly.

Although native to coastlines in the Southern Hemisphere,

the forests of giant kelp fringe only one coastline in the Northern Hemisphere, an exception credited to the ice age. Kelp abhors tepid water; the ice age apparently provided the chill that enabled kelp from the west coast of South America to bound across the equator and colonize the western rim of North America.

The abundant life within a sea forest stems from kelp's "biomass" capability. Biomass is the amount of living matter per unit of area. A kelp plant, with its many fronds, injects far more living matter into a given area than the ocean's tiny, current-driven microalgae, plankton. By providing food and shelter, kelp forests sustain far more life than a rock reef. Up to 90,000 juvenile fish may exist in less than half a hectare of kelp forest. Even in death, marine plants sustain life. Drift kelp encrusted with juicy organisms becomes a prime food source for bottom feeders and for inshore marine communities.

To understand how kelp and other seaweeds gain their energy, you have to turn landside botany upside down. The blades extract nutrients from the surrounding water instead of the seabed. The nutrients travel down the tubular stipes to nourish new growth at the holdfast base. Special blades at the base release trillions of seedlike spores, which can attach to the seabed and grow into mature plants.

As biomass champ of the ocean, giant kelp becomes a forest in the ocean, a splendid sanctuary for marine life, a submarine playground for divers, and a bountiful fishing ground. One day, on poking my head through the kelp canopy, I discovered another thriving human activity: An ungainly barge was lumbering along, its deck piled high with kelp.

The kelp industry emerged after a heated diplomatic exchange. In 1910, Germany enjoyed a world monopoly on deposits of potash, an important fertilizer. When Germany rejected an American claim that potash prices were being rigged, the U.S. Congress authorized the Department of Agriculture to uncover domestic sources. That kelp contains acetone, a critical compound in ammunition, helped spur the search. That kelp blades remove potassium, a prime base of potash, from the ocean qualified sea forests off southern California as a potential source of potash. A dozen prospective kelp-harvesting companies sprang up. Many were better prepared to bilk eager investors than to harvest kelp. Fishermen complained that kelp harvesting, however accomplished, would scatter fish communities. Beach residents grumbled that cut kelp would litter their front yards. Germany reacted to all this activity by becoming more flexible in potash negotiations, but World War I terminated this flexibility. The sea forests were drafted into the war effort. Men in rowboats yanked the kelp from its holdfast, tug-of-war fashion, so that it would wash ashore. Burning reduced it to potash. The Hercules Powder Company mechanized this crude process by outfitting barges with cutter blades and harvesting the kelp like hay. The kelp was then fermented in large vats. In a year's time, 3,500 tons of potash were recovered from 305,000 tons of kelp. Although kelp harvesting did not realize the fears of fishermen and beach residents, its fermentation left an indelible impression. "There came galloping out to meet us, before we even got to the outpost, a smell that would cause women to faint and strong men to hesitate. It didn't smell like anything else in the world, but once smelled it is never forgotten," explained one visitor.

At war's end, harvesting slowed to a crawl, but a new era in prepared foods, premixed medicines, and synthetic products was dawning. Dampness was disintegrating aspirin, packaged ice cream, and other harbingers of the new era, and a chemical fastener, or stabilizer, was required. Kelco Company of San Diego, a survivor of the kelp depression, found that a particular compound in kelp endowed the fronds with a tensile strength that allowed them to withstand the constant wave surge. An extract from this compound, algin, kept ice cream together without affecting flavor, color, weight, or cost. Today, algin suspends, stabilizes, gel-produces, and emulsifies laxatives, penicillin, candy, and some 300 other products. The sea forests off southern California thus ensure that the synthetic age will not collapse.

Besides pioneering in ocean exploitation, the kelp industry has pioneered in its conservation. The industry has volunteered to pay increased fees to the California Fish and Game Department, which leases the forests as a property of the state, to underwrite enforcement of harvesting regulations. The mechanized barges that sweep through the kelp like hay reapers must cut only to a depth of four feet so that the forests can regenerate. Because kelp has difficulty surviving in warm water and dies when the water temperature goes above seventy-five degrees Fahrenheit, harvesting may be restricted during critical warm spells.

The reproductive capacity of the kelp, the foresight of the kelp industry, and the prized recreational allure of the forests would seem to preclude destruction. Yet the sea forests off southern California have been faced with just such a prospect. By the late 1940s, harvesters had to make longer and more costly runs to reach healthy kelp stands. By the late 1950s, the Palos Verdes forest off Los Angeles, once three square miles in size, was a virtual marine desert. In a visit there, I found myself roaming through a ghost forest, strangely somnolent except for stray perch or a clutch of leafless, stringy fronds.

Fishermen, along with skin divers and beach residents, blamed overzealous kelp harvesters for the recession. Kelp harvesters blamed a proliferation of coastal sewage outfalls. An ocean poorly understood lends itself to heated exchanges.

During the 1960s, Dr. Wheeler North, a scuba-diving biologist now with the California Institute of Technology, noticed that an animal resembling a purple pincushion remained in the ghost forests. Sea urchins normally graze on kelp and then move on. Like cattle lingering on a dusty pasture, the stationary urchins appeared to prevent a kelp recovery.

Could the ghost forests be revived if urchins—"spiny locusts" in the press—were eliminated? Volunteer divers descended with hammers to crush urchins, but this approach was too slow. One day, a miniature snowstorm descended on urchins in a receded kelp forest off San Diego. The snow consisted of caustic lime. Young kelp plants soon began sprouting up among the dead urchins. Would new urchins migrate in to devour the reviving kelp? The kelp grew fast enough to satiate urchin appetites with drift kelp. As the kelp returned, so did abalone, sheephead, scuba divers, and kelp harvesters.

To revive the barren Palos Verdes area, biologist Ken Wilson of the California Department of Fish and Game would pry up plants whole from healthy beds, place them in burlap bags aboard a vessel, and then lace the holdfasts to anchor chains on the Palos Verdes bottom. Grazers nibbled away at an initial transplant. More than 4,000 plants were imported to satiate the nibblers.

Under the care of the underwater rangers, kelp off Palos Verdes expanded from 1.42 acres in 1974 to 899 acres by 1990. The kelp can recede during coastal storms and periods of warm water but recovers within a year's time, according to Fish and Game biologist Heidi Togstad. The area now provides transplants for other restoration sites, including Los Angeles Harbor.

Ironically, scientists are unable to pinpoint the sequence of events behind either the kelp's revival or its decline. As cooler waters returned, some beds recovered without the aid of a single transplant or liming. Urban sewage remains one suspect in the original decline. Some scientists feel that sewage particles reduce energy-giving light penetration. By accumulating on the bottom, the particles may also snuff out young plants. Kelp now grows near coastal outfalls that have reduced their particulate sewage load to comply with federal regulations. Outfall discharges of DDT have also been reduced, primarily at the Los Angeles County Whites Point outfall off Palos Verdes (the largest single sewage discharge in California). DDT, already linked to reproductive failure in brown pelicans, could be toxic to kelp spores, according to Dr. Alan Mearns, a scientist with the National

Oceanographic and Atmospheric Administration (NOAA). Other scientists believe that removal of key urchin predators may lead to urchin population explosions and to overgrazing. Fur hunters in the nineteenth century decimated the sea otter, one major urchin predator. By the 1950s, when the kelp decline became severe, spiny lobster, sheephead, and other urchin predators were being depleted by both fishermen and scuba divers. These natural urchin control agents have yet to regain their former abundance. (A fishery has emerged in California to remove urchins for export to Japan, which considers urchin gonads a delicacy. But the purple urchin—the most formidable kelp grazer—is not the preferred species.)

In 1991, a side effect from nuclear power generation was damaging a kelp bed near San Clemente, California. The San Onofre power plant discharges seawater used to cool its reactors. The turbid discharge restricts light and cuts growth in the kelp bed by 60 percent, stated a committee reporting to the California Coastal Commission. The plant's seawater intake also entraps and kills an estimated 57 tons of fish a year.

The fate of giant kelp personifies the changing public image of seaweed. Once regarded as a nuisance on the beach, then subjected to unwitting exploitation, the monster seaweed now emerges as a million-dollar resource and a key ecological element that must be carefully studied and monitored if we expect to reap the full benefits of the living oceans. Prudent use can prevent costly ecological backlashes. Restore a depleted big-game fish and you restore its stock alone. Restore a marine algae community and you help retrieve a whole spectrum of marine life, from the diving seabirds above to the gangly lobster below, as well as helping to revive the fortunes of commercial fishermen, sport anglers, skin divers, and seaweed harvesters.

In Puget Sound, Washington, state marine biologist Tom Mumford is working to restore another large kelp, bull kelp. Herring spawn their eggs on the blades of this kelp. Herring roe on kelp is exported to Japan, where it is considered a delicacy.

By restoring this kelp, Mumford will augment the lucrative harvest. The harvest is now controlled to protect both the bull kelp and the herring stocks.

The fate of the kelp forests triggered my interest in the fate of other marine algae communities throughout the world. Hawaii may eat through some of its seaweed resources. Native Hawaiians once had no onions, peppers, or tomatoes to spice up an otherwise uniform diet of poi (pounded taro) and fish. Lumu—seaweeds—that were drafted to fill this nutritional void provided key vitamins, too. Hawaii's immigrant groups stepped up the demand for edible seaweeds. Today, one popular seaweed, the crisp-textured, red-colored ogo, can fetch $3.00 a pound. Local supplies have been stressed by mounting market demand, silt runoff, and habitat destruction. A reef runway at the Honolulu jetport obliterated one popular seaweed patch. Inexperienced pickers can yank up a whole plant, ruining its ability to regenerate. Hawaiian conservation officials encourage pickers to pinch off only the top portion of the plant. Two local firms now grow ogo in seawater tanks onshore; the ogo growers plan to market their crunchy product in mainland markets, too.

Dr. Maxwell Doty of the University of Hawaii is becoming the Johnny Appleseed of the Pacific Basin. He teaches Filipino and Polynesian coastal communities to raise a red alga, *Eucheuma*, on nets set in coral atolls. *Eucheuma* buyers show up from Europe and the United States. A *Eucheuma* extract—carrageen—keeps the chocolate in chocolate milk in suspension. Weight watchers may receive a surprise dividend from carrageen. An international fast-food chain, McDonald's, is test-marketing a low-calorie burger that features a combination of lean meat, with carrageen added to provide the moisture normally supplied in fat.

Japan's passion for seaweed rivals that of Hawaii. Long before the term *aquaculture* became fashionable, Japanese coastal villagers were learning to cultivate nori, an alga often sold in purple-colored pressed sheets. These pioneer sea farmers first grew young plants on bamboo stakes and then shifted them to nets laid horizontally above the shallow seabed.

In 1949, England's Dr. Kathleen Drew identified the microscopic spore-producing phase of *Porphyra,* the plant source for nori. This discovery enabled the Japanese to "seed" their nets and extend production into deeper, less polluted waters. Whereas in 1947 Japan produced about 860 million sheets of nori, today, thanks in part to Dr. Drew's research, Japan produces seven *billion* sheets annually. Nori culture, the country's largest single inshore marine fishery, is now a billion-dollar-a-year industry. Japan's best-selling pizza comes with—you guessed it—a topping of nori.

Many Americans eat nori without realizing it. The dark green wrapper around rice rolls served in Japanese-style sushi bars is nori. Biologist Tom Mumford of Washington State's Department of Natural Resources has noticed that Seattle stores are selling nori imported from Japan, even though native stocks flourish in nearby Puget Sound. "With sushi bars becoming so popular, the United States imports about $6 million worth of nori from Japan each year," says Mumford, who developed a nori demonstration farm in Puget Sound. Based on this research, a Seattle scientist-turned-businessman, John Merrill, is developing North America's first commercial nori farm in British Columbia. Across the continent, in Nova Scotia, another small red seaweed, Irish moss, is being raised in tanks onshore as a source of carrageen, the emulsifier used in chocolate milk.

Because of its culturing efforts on brown seaweed (*Laminaria*), China today is a leading producer of seaweed—more than $300 million worth annually. Seaweed farmers enjoy major advantages over their landside counterparts. They don't worry about soil erosion, drought, or tract developers. Nor are expensive fertilizers needed; the surrounding sea provides the basic nutrients. Commercial fish farms, such as salmon pens, can pollute surrounding waters with fecal and feed wastes. Seaweed farms, by taking up nutrients in the water column, can actually improve water quality. At Oregon's Hatfield Marine Science Center, researchers John-Eric Levin and William McNeil have found that algal rearing tanks can be used to clean up nutrient-rich waste streams generated by salmon culture operations. "Seaweed farmers do have to worry about storm damage, oil spills, sewage plumes, and abnormal water temperatures," notes Heidi Togstad of the California Department of Fish and Game.

The plant that first revealed to me the charms of seaweed inspires visions of ocean energy farms. The Gas Research Institute (GRI) in Chicago, supported by private natural gas companies, has studied giant kelp as one biomass fuel candidate. GRI has sponsored experimental kelp plantings off the California coast. A steel submarine trellis, required to support one deep-water kelp farm, was lost in a storm.

Other marine biomass candidates include *Gracilaria,* the source of ogo, and free-floating *Sargassum,* the namesake for the Sargasso Sea in the mid-Atlantic. Unlike giant kelp, these smaller algae do not require costly support structures. Marine biomass candidates have a major advantage over such landside candidates as sugarcane and wood—the ocean offers more growing space at less cost. In 1991, the crisis in the Middle East and the political price of oil served to renew interest in marine biomass research.

Europe has been more concerned over unwanted seaweed invasions. In 1973, France's Institut Scientifique et Technique des Pêches Maritimes (ISTPM) was experimenting with imported giant kelp in coastal Brittany. ISTPM wanted to develop a new alginate source. But some British scientists feared the alien algae would colonize the United Kingdom, drive out native algae, and upset natural marine ecosystems. According to Gerald Boalch of the Marine Biological Association, "The records of where man has introduced aquatic plants from one area to another all indicate that the immigrant has got out of control and caused problems." To the British Admiralty, runaway kelp could become a navigation hazard. The French researchers decided to culture a smaller, less intimidating species of seaweed.

At the Marine Science Institute of the University of California at Santa Barbara, Dr. Michael Neushul has worked to develop high-yield kelp hybrids. Hybrids, which are generally sterile, can eliminate the uncontrolled spread of introduced, or "foreign," plants. "It is certainly worthwhile to explore the potential of marine plants as collectors of energy and concentrators of nutrients," Neushul says. "They may contribute significantly to a solar-based world food-and-energy production system."

Like our forests on land, our marine forests can last forever— with proper study and care. Our magnificent seaweed heritage, in "wild" sea forests and ocean energy food farms, may prove to be an important part of our future on this watery planet.

CHAPTER TWO

Are We Fishing Too Far Down the Food Chain?

Fishermen call it a "boil." The blue sea starts to froth as if it were boiling. As the boil moves slowly along the horizon, a pelican materializes out of a deserted sky. It hovers for a moment, then plunges seaward to penetrate the source of the boil: a huge school of small, silvery fish. Their wriggling bodies make the ocean surface froth. The pelican pops back to the surface, its pouchlike bill filled with some of the wriggling bodies. The one pelican is followed by a hundred, the hundred by a thousand hovering, diving, splashing, gorging pelicans. Screeching seagulls join this aerial circus to compete for scraps that fall from the pelicans' bills.

Other predators converge on the boil from below: the sleek, torpedolike forms of tuna and barracuda. The tuna attempt to encircle the school so that the tight formation will turn into panic-stricken chaos. Sharks displace the gorging tuna and barracuda and then blindly bite one another as the feeding frenzy spirals. Blood streaks the boil.

Caught between seabirds above and marine predators below, the small fish continue to move as one unit, twisting and veering, moving up and down, trying to shake their tormentors. The school will succeed and survive out of sheer abundance. The seabirds, tuna, barracuda, and sharks eventually recede. The sea is blue again.

Today, a new predator stalks these telltale boils with huge walls of webbing. The global fishing industry, which once used boils as clues to bigger fish, now pursues the smaller fish, too. And it does so with a relentless efficiency that could jeopardize the living oceans.

The boil is a critical link in the marine food chain. Large land animals—such as buffalo, elephants, deer, and horses—forage on mountain meadows and prairies. The ocean contains few equivalent large forage plant systems, yet it teems with life. Marine pastures are formed by tiny plants and animals—plankton—that drift with the currents. Baleen, or filter-feeding, whales graze on these mobile pastures, but most large marine animals can't. Instead, they must pursue the small, filter-feeding fish found in the boils—sardine, anchovy, menhaden, herring, and related species. (Scientists group these fish into the suborder clupeoids.)

If such a food chain prevailed on land, elephants and buffalo might pursue rodent packs, which in turn would pursue tiny plants drifting across the landscape like dust clouds. Without forage fish, our most esteemed sport and commercial fish would be on short rations. Forage fish are thus valuable to us even without being caught. As a prime food source for marine animals higher in the food chain, forage fish play a key role in the global marine ecosystem. They challenge our ability to carefully understand how our exploitive ambitions can reverberate throughout this ecosystem.

Forage fish appear to reproduce as haphazardly as a dandelion giving up its tiny seeds to summer breezes. On moonlit nights, a female menhaden may emit up to 10,000 eggs. In a year's time, this female may emit up to 700,000 eggs. The hatched young, smaller than your thumbnail, enter a hostile world with few natural defenses. They cannot sting, bite, poison, or outswim predators. Squirrels and other small land animals can scamper up trees or down burrows; the open ocean offers few sanctuaries. Adults do not protect their struggling young. Indeed, adults may consume their progeny amid the plankton pastures. The young destined to survive will form a crucial elite. From 50 to 99 percent of the eggs that are spawned will not survive to adulthood.

After consuming their yolk sac, the newborn fish literally collide with their first meal of tiny marine plants and animals. With this newfound energy, the minute fish sense their power to guide themselves. The body deepens. Scales form. A remarkable evolutionary imprint asserts itself. Without milling about or bumping into one another, the tiny fish begin to move together as one. They may form a school less than three months after being cast randomly into the waters.

By schooling, the small fish can band together as one large object to scare off smaller predators. Once under attack, the school's outer members may satiate predator appetites and spare most of the school's other members. One school can be as wide as three football fields and as deep as ninety feet, and it can contain a population of millions. These millions of fish swim with a close precision that a Marine drill instructor could appreciate.

Forage fish can swim with their mouths agape, filtering two gallons of water a minute to extract their microscopic diet. At every aquatic turn, these marathon feeders can face stabbing beaks or ripping teeth. Forage fish grow a foot long and weigh six pounds, but most are as long and as light as your pen. They can live six years or longer, but few will die of old age. Their final resting place is often the stomach of a tuna, seal, or seabird. They are universal fodder, as critical to marine life systems as prairies and meadows are to life systems on land.

People close to the sea have sensed this relationship for some time. In 1556, four centuries before the advent of marine ecologists and environmental impact reports, the Dutch painter Pieter Brueghel depicted a huge, beached fish in one of his paintings. Men on ladders were cutting open the fish's belly. Out of the belly and the mouth spilled a glut of small fish. The painting was entitled *Big Fish Eat Little Fish*.

Human beings have also exploited select forage stocks as food. The Pacific sardine off California, as a cheap source of canned protein, helped millions of Americans survive the Great Depression. The anchovy has livened up countless pizzas. For more than three centuries, the North Sea herring has served as a protein staple for millions of Europeans. British herring fishermen would chant:

> We who plow the North Sea deep
> Though never sowing, always reap
> The harvest which to all is free.

Other forage stocks were considered too oily and not as tasty as tuna, salmon, and other preferred species. Scorned by the civilized palate, clupeoids often wound up as fertilizer or bait. As a boy fishing on California sport charter boats, I encountered the burning question concerning the northern anchovy: should it be hooked through the mouth or the tail in order to catch "real" fish?

A shift in world food production transformed forage fish into gold mines of the sea. Since World War II, poultry and pig ranchers have used artificial feeds instead of household garbage to expand production. Feed supplements must be cheap, nutritious, and in ample supply. Forage fish ground up into fish meal can serve this purpose.

To serve as animal feed, forage fish must be caught in quantities far in excess of fish caught for human consumption. One ton of fish meal requires five tons of forage fish. In one year, Peru surpassed such fishing giants as Russia and Japan in tons of fish landed by catching twelve million metric tons of just one fish, the six-inch-long anchoveta. The twelve million tons became less than three million tons of meal.

The schooling behavior that wards off natural predation assists such massive human predation. By schooling, forage fish do everything but swim into the fishing vessel and operate the machinery. Sardine and herring schools become mobile veins of biological ore, to be detected by electronic probes and extracted by walls of webbing. The telltale boils help alert eager fishermen to their presence. And schools show up clearly on sonar screens even when they're well below the sea surface.

A huge net is deployed around the sonar "signature." Whirring winches retrieve it and tighten it into a sodden bag of tiny, writhing bodies whose scales flash silver under night-work lights. A suction hose transfers this squirming cargo to the hold. One school can contain up to 10,000 tons of "raw" product, and one cast of a mechanized net can retrieve more than 200 tons. We could not train these fish to fit so perfectly our industrial needs.

Because the tons of wet biomass sloshing around in the holds of a hunter-vessel would overwhelm a conventional cannery, a special reduction plant is required. This kind of plant, with its metal stacks, looping pipes, and storage tanks, resembles a refinery or mine smelter. You smell a reduction plant before you see it. Indeed, the most accurate set of directions I ever received came while in search of one in coastal New Jersey: "Just follow the stink."

Forage fish that enter this plant in huge suction hoses depart in limp brown bags of meal. Inside, machinery steam-cooks, presses, dries, and grinds tons of fish—heads, bones, guts, and all—into a tan-colored, powdery meal. One steam cooker can cook thirty-five tons every hour. Oil squeezed out of the lifeless bodies helps to make margarine, lipstick, and explosives. There is not much left for scavenging cats and gulls.

Through such industrial ingenuity, one critical element in the marine food system can be diverted to barnyards thousands of miles away from the sound of foghorns and bell buoys. Six-pound chickens and 200-pound hogs can gorge themselves on marine protein snatched from the jaws of tuna and the bills of pelicans. Our own dietary preferences fuel this massive protein diversion. Each American consumes about 60 pounds of fish yearly, but 75 percent of this is consumed in the form of eggs, chicken, ham, and sausage from poultry and pigs nourished in part on fish meal.

Everybody would appear to benefit by fishing further down the food chain: the poultry producers and consumers, the fishermen, the coastal-hamlets-turned-fishing-boomtowns. Governments will even subsidize construction of fishing fleets to cash in on the commercial clamor for clupeoids. Fish-meal exports can secure sorely needed foreign exchange for nations battling trade deficits. Peru has obtained up to one-third of its foreign exchange by pursuing the anchoveta.

The case for exploiting the gold mines of the sea seems persuasive until you consider the economic and ecological backlash. Just how abundant are these fish? How great is the danger of disrupting the food chain?

Our exploitation of forage stocks was producing disturbing results even before the global demand for fish meal skyrocketed. During the 1930s, the largest fishery in the United States flourished off California. Its target: the Pacific sardine. Catches began to fluctuate dramatically by the 1940s. By the 1950s, the Monterey canneries immortalized by John Steinbeck began closing. Scavenging gulls moved on to rotting garbage dumps and other new food sources.

Some scientists expected the sardine to rebound. But other nations hurried to build up their own forage fisheries to cash in on California's misfortune and profit from the fish-meal boom. Fishing vessels were built to travel faster. Nets were made larger. Airplane spotters were recruited to expand a vessel's range of detection. Fish schools show up like inkblots from the air, and the spotter can direct the set of the net with the precision of an artillery spotter bracketing gunfire.

Some idle California canners were surprised to find that Spanish-speaking businessmen were anxious to buy their rusting equipment. The buyers were gearing up to exploit the Peruvian anchoveta.

Because of the frenetic global hunt for forage fish, the world marine fish catch soared, growing in annual jumps of 8 percent. But in the 1970s, the catch leveled off, growing at 2 percent or less a year.

What happened?

During the late 1960s and early 1970s, the forage fisheries declined abruptly: herring and menhaden catches off our Atlantic Coast, the herring fishery off Norway, the sardine fishery off South Africa. "The harvest which to all is free"—the North Sea herring fishery—plummeted, unable to feed both human beings and livestock. The traditional chant of herring fishermen became a bitter parody.

Scientists refer to these spectacular declines as population collapses, or crashes—and no wonder. Peru's anchoveta fishery went from a record twelve million metric tons in 1970 to less than two million metric tons by 1973. For Peru, the massive buildup of the fishing industry became an economic curse. Reduction plants became as useless as smelters next to a played-out mine. In California, some sardine canneries have reopened—as restored theme restaurants that import marine entrees from as far away as South Africa.

Such collapses can stun marine scientists as well as coastal communities and political leaders. Describing the anchoveta collapse as "another clupeoid misadventure," U.S. fishery expert Garth Murphy concluded, "Clearly, something is wrong with our approach to these kinds of resources."

What accounts for such collapses? Because of natural causes, forage fish populations fluctuate much more dramatically from year to year than tuna and other stocks higher on the food chain. Just a few degrees' difference in water temperature or a change in ocean currents can result in a poor year for survival of newborn fish. The population usually bounces back, however, once favorable climatic conditions return.

That's why some scientists expected the Pacific sardine to recover quickly. But it didn't. Had overfishing, on top of unfavorable climatic conditions, triggered the collapse? In 1967, almost two decades after the sardine collapse, California decided to ban sardine fishing at the behest of scientists. Few sardine fishermen were left to protest.

Fishery advisers who once urged Peru to intensively fish the anchoveta now urged caution. But to Peru, as to other nations before and since, the clupeoid collapses were an economic goad rather than an ecological omen. World fish-meal prices were soaring.

In 1972, two years after the record anchoveta catch, Peru's coastal waters became warmer. Heavy rains triggered floods that rampaged through coastal boomtowns. Fishing vessels returned to port with empty holds. The fishery and Peru's economy were in the hot, humid grip of El Niño. Cooler waters have long since returned, but not the anchoveta in its former abundance. Peru's experience confirmed what many scientists first began to suspect in California: Overfishing on top of poor climatic conditions can trigger forage fishery collapses.

Today, fishermen who exceed catch limits on North Sea herring may be jailed or fined. Such penalties seek to ensure recovery of marine gold mines. With such protection, depleted predator stocks like salmon, halibut, and certain marine mammal species can recover in some cases. What about depleted forage stocks? The Pacific sardine shows signs of limited recovery some forty years after being intensively exploited. No one is predicting whether this stock, along with the North Sea herring, the Norwegian herring, the Peruvian anchoveta, and the South African sardine, will ever regain its former abundance. By the late 1980s, three more forage fish stocks—the Gulf of California sardine in Mexico, an anchovy shared by France and Spain, and the capelin in the Barents Sea—joined the ranks of the overfished. When we risk fishing further down the marine food chain, we may get only one roll of the dice.

And we can lose more than forage fish with a bad roll. When Peru's anchoveta declined, so did a major anchoveta predator— the bonito, which is similar to the tuna. For a nation reeling from the loss of its major export, this related decline was another economic blow. The bonito was Peru's major domestic food fish. Peru's seabird population also declined, from twenty-eight million to a low of a half-million. Ergo, another economic setback. Guano (bird droppings) deposited on desert islets by these anchoveta predators supplies a fertilizer industry.

Why are seabirds so vulnerable to such collapses? Pelican expert James Keith of the U.S. Fish and Wildlife Service observes that a pelican, when feeding by itself, will recover a fish on fewer than half its dives. With a boil, or "pileup," this success rate jumps to 90 percent. "It is not the biomass of fish in the ocean, but the pileup which is important for the pelican," says Keith. Alternative prey that could sustain fish predators may swim at depths beyond a seabird's diving capability.

The fate of a small fish off the New England shore adds another foreboding dimension to such collapses. The sand lance is so named because it will plunge into the sandy seabed to evade bluefish, porpoises, and other predators. While Atlantic herring stocks have receded under exploitation, sand lance stocks have proliferated. (At low tide, clam diggers will see these fish clustered like huge piles of silver ore.) Is this shift just a coincidence? The two species compete for similar food sources, including their own young. Some scientists now feel that the sand lance population can expand as its food competitors are removed. Furthermore, its expanded population can serve as a lid to retard recovery of the stressed stock. According to the National Oceanic and Atmospheric Administration (NOAA), the sand lance "may significantly impair the ability of herring stocks to return to their former levels."

Our fishing strategies thus not only can exhaust a forage stock but can militate against its recovery by altering the very composition of a coastal ecosystem. Do stocks favored by such selective fishing pressures provide the basis for new gold mines of the sea? Replacement species are often smaller, shorter-lived species with less economic value. According to the NOAA, the sand lance is a "smaller, less economically desirable species." Other less desirable species—skates and dogfish—become more numerous in the stressed New England marine ecosystem as their particular competitors—cod and other groundfish—suffer from overfishing. If we gardened like we fish, we would uproot vegetables so that crabgrass could expand.

Clearly, we must either recognize the critical role of forage fish or risk disrupting the marine ecosystem and our own expectations of the ocean as a protein source. The pelican skimming along the waves, the seal sunning itself on a rock, the tuna cruising in the blue depths, and the anchovy school swimming just below the surface may appear to have separate fates; but in reality, their fates are inextricably intertwined. Yet we tend to manage each fish species separately. We assign catch quotas, or limits, on a species-by-species basis with little or no regard either for the complex ways that fish interact with one another or for climatic changes. Imagine what would happen if we managed a cattle herd without regard for the condition of the range.

Scientists now urge that fishery resources be managed on a multispecies, or ecosystem, basis. Congress recognized this need in passing the landmark Fisheries Conservation and Management Act (FCMA) in 1976. This act extends our fishery jurisdiction 200 miles seaward to control foreign fishing efforts. Realizing that domestic fishing must also be controlled, Congress mandated that the secretary of commerce, through the National Marine Fisheries Service (NMFS) and regional fishery councils, prepare management plans. These plans must "prevent overfishing" and "rebuild overfished stocks." The act declares that "interrelated stocks of fish shall be managed as a unit or in close coordination" and that the secretary of commerce shall maintain a "comprehensive program" of "biological research concerning the interdependence of fisheries or stocks of fish."

Despite such strong admonitions, fish stocks continue to suffer from inadequate management and overfishing. In a 1990 report to Congress, the National Fish and Wildlife Foundation reported, "A major reason for the poor state of U.S. fisheries is the regional councils' tendency to set catch levels that are more attuned to the economic needs of fishermen than to the long-term conservation of the stocks." The foundation also criticized Congress and the executive branch for failing to provide NMFS with the funds necessary to do adequate research and to enforce its regulations. "NMFS has been seriously underfunded and understaffed for years," noted the foundation report. The report recommended increasing the funding level by $60 million a year to enable NMFS to meet congressional goals. But overriding problems with the federal budget continue to restrict NMFS's ability to properly husband the nation's living marine resources.

At the same time, a new pressure to catch more forage fish for animal feed emerges. As the catch of wild marine fish stocks levels off or declines, fish farmers benefit by boosting their production. Like pig and chicken farmers, they use fish-fortified feeds to raise their captive salmon, yellowtail, catfish, and trout. To meet growth projections for cage-farmed salmon in Norway in the 1990s, some 430,000 more tons of forage fish a year— equivalent to 15 percent of the North Sea's total fish production—will have to be caught, according to marine ecologists Nils Kautsky and Carl Folke of the University of Stockholm. "Increasing exploitation of fish-prey species used as feed for aquaculture may cause decreases in commercially important fish stocks such as cod or tuna, and thereby decrease the economic returns from conventional fisheries," warn the pair in a 1989 article for *Ambio.*

Pressures to fish further down the food chain may jeopardize the existence of the ocean's largest living creatures. In the Southern Ocean, which encircles Antarctica, swarms of small, shrimplike krill sustain what large whales remain. They also are key to the food web that sustains countless seals, penguins, seabirds, and finfish. Japan and the Soviet Union now pursue the krill for fishmeal and for use as a shrimp substitute. The 1980 Convention on the Conservation of Antarctic Marine Living Resources establishes conservation of the the marine ecosystem and its biodiversity as the basic management goal. Like the NMFS, however, the scientific committee responsible for developing ecosystem safeguards has lacked the resources to adequately research such a dynamic and wide-ranging ecosystem. Moreover, management actions have to wait on a consensus of the fishing nations; some species, including the Antarctic cod, have already been overfished. The krill catch, which increased sixfold during the 1980s, now constitutes 78 percent of the total Antarctic catch. In 1991, the Soviets and the Japanese blocked adoption of a precautionary cap on the krill catch, as proposed by the scientific committee. Significant numbers of juvenile fish are being killed by krill trowls.

Sidney Holt, a fisheries adviser to the United Nations' Food and Agricultural Organization, has warned that it might be prudent "to leave the Southern Ocean in its relatively pristine state for the time being, while the great whales recover, while mankind learns much more about the dynamics of that rich biological system, and while strong international institutions are developed which would one day be capable of organizing a rational use of the area for the benefit of mankind." In 1991, a global coalition of environmental groups was working to establish Antarctica and its surrounding seas as an international reserve that would be off-limits to oil and mineral development.

In a world of more than five billion people, we must also think long and hard about the waste of marine protein that occurs when fish are converted to livestock feed. As U.S. nutrition expert Dr. Jean Mayer has observed, "More food would be provided man if a smaller percentage were used as animal feed." If the U.S. menhaden fishery were diverted from animal feed to human food, U.S. supplies of edible fish would double. The NMFS has been exploring the feasibility of making surimi— imitation seafoods—from menhaden. California is permitting a limited harvest on the Pacific sardine, but only for use in direct human consumption; sardines can not be used for reduction purposes.

Would this shift away from fishmeal put the livestock industry on short rations? Ranchers have already learned to rely on other feeds—soybeans, cottonseed meal, meat scraps—that can be cheaper and in more dependable supply. As a result, poultry production can continue to expand while the forage fish catch declines or stagnates.

By more efficient use of existing fisheries, we could gain time to develop more reliable fishery management plans and give our coastal species a better chance to recover from past mistakes. When we overfish the small forage fish of the sea, we tinker with a critical link in the marine life system. We had better know what we are doing.

CHAPTER THREE

Leaving Room for Whales

In the coastal lagoons of Baja California, you can encounter a unique obstacle to carefree navigation. In the near distance, a glistening, rubbery hull rends the calm waters, spouts a minor geyser of condensed breath, and slips silently back beneath the blue cover of the desert lagoon. Without warning, but fifteen yards away, a sonorous exhalation sounds, like the whoosh of a steam press, and a blowhole, spewing like a volcanic island, emerges. A cloud of vapor vanishes, exposing two dark pits that mark the nostrils. A long, grayish black hull encrusted with knobby barnacles trails the submerging blowhole. You watch, amazed, as the mere backbone of a whale instantly cuts everything down to size. Then, to the rear, a smaller blowhole emerges. A newborn calf mimics the lead of its mother.

The whale species you are watching, the gray, lacks the celebrity credentials of the giant blue, the singing humpback, or the intrepid orca (a.k.a. "killer" whale). But the gray has its own claim to fame. Because of its vulnerability to human activity, the gray has become a major bellwether of (a) the ability of

whales to endure in an age of intense marine exploitation and
(b) our own ability to help ensure survival.

Baja California dangles boldly from the southwestern extreme
of North America, a geological dagger that plunges into the
Pacific and splits the ocean apart from the Gulf of California
and northern Mexico. What attracts the gray—a large whale
species forty tons in weight and up to fifty feet in length—to the
desert lagoons of this rugged peninsula? One major lagoon,
Scammon, is big enough to accommodate the 6,000 or so whales
that come annually; a two-mile-wide ocean entrance expands
into a body of water some thirty-five miles long, eleven miles
wide, and twenty feet deep.

This vast body of water resembles a biblical sea that would
merge with the sky except for a thin desert horizon. Yet the
lagoon generally remains as placid as its counterpart in a municipal park. This quality can be important to a pregnant whale,
which must teach its one-ton baby to breathe and swim immediately. The lagoon's high salinity—twice that of the open
ocean—provides another benefit, added buoyancy.

Eelgrass beds may be another attraction. Some scientists believe that the gray can scoop up these beds, filter them through
its brushlike baleen to expel mud, and thus retain shellfish and
other morsels. The lagoon offers seclusion, too. Human intrusion has caused the gray to desert some calving grounds. In
Scammon, the grays have enjoyed a natural solitude protected
by the lagoon's remoteness—at least up to the present.

The lagoon visitors come all the way from their choice feeding
grounds in the Arctic Ocean, a migration of some 5,000 miles,
or 10,000 round-trip. (A smaller herd summers in the Sea of
Okhotsk and winters in the bays of southern Korea. The gray
became extinct in the North Atlantic in the 1700s, possibly
because of overexploitation by Basque and Yankee whalers.)
Despite their massive bulk, restricted vision (whales can't see
their tails), and impotent sense of smell, the grays make this
magnificent migration year after year. To overcome such defi-
ciencies, the gray utilizes a batlike sense of hearing and organic

sonar (echo sounding) that enables it to "see" through sound and navigate the northern Pacific Ocean. Whale hydrodynamics consists of an economy of motion. The huge bulk is streamlined into an elongated exclamation point with such friction-free features as recessed nipples, ears, and reproductive organs. With its nostrils on top of its head, the whale never has to thrust its ponderous head out of the water to breathe. The whale's flukes, or fan-shaped paddle, drive this streamlined body at speeds as high as 15 fifteen knots—a good pace for any large ship.

Equipped with a keen sense of hearing, superb hydrodynamics, and organic food storage, the Arctic-grazing grays head for their desert birthplace in mid-September, followed for a short time by white snowbirds that gorge on their leavings. The grays are a loose, straggling lot in migration, separated by miles of ocean and weeks of time. In the lead are the pregnant females, which set a pace of about a hundred miles a day. This informal procession passes through the Chukchi and Bering seas before the cold waters stiffen to ice, loops around the Aleutian Islands, and trails along the coast of British Columbia. Occasionally, some migrants rub their barnacle-encrusted torsos against the anchor chains of a Canadian lightship.

By November, the procession passes within sight of Cape Flattery, a lonely headland in Washington State. Countless blows, or "plumes," form rainbow prisms in the light of the ocean sun. Soon after, those sailing out of San Francisco can watch certain whales exchange taps with their front stabilizer flippers. These exchanges between males and eligible females are regarded as love taps. They resound for miles.

Occasionally, a group of grays will hastily meld into a giant, revolving pinwheel with their limber tails as spokes. This formation wards off wolflike packs of toothed killer whales (orcas). That is another lagoon attraction: an absence of swift orcas.

By late December, this rainbow-plumed procession tightens up and passes in review off Point Loma, a San Diego headland. About 300 miles south of Point Loma and three weeks later, the lead pregnant whales come within echo sounding of submerged

sandbars. "No definite directions can be given for crossing the
bar at Scammon, which is constantly changing," notes the U.S.
Navy Hydrographic Office. Like phantom beaches, these submerged bars transform swells into surf. The grays, with a draft
of six to eight feet, thread their way through the submerged
obstacle course to enter their calm calving grounds.

The grays have three major breeding lagoons along Baja's
Pacific side—San Ignacio, the lagoon channels in Magdalena
Bay, and Scammon. Scammon attracts some 6,000; their con-
stant blows endow the lagoon with a built-in sprinkler system.

Sometimes a whale's mighty forward torso will shoot out of
the water like a metal pile and then topple in an explosion of
foam; this maneuver is called "breaching." Another whale will
emerge from the lagoon depths in what is called a "spy hop" as
casually as a cobra from a basket. Here the whale's lower jaw
unhinges like a drawbridge, and the desert sky becomes pin-
ioned in the creature's open mouth. The jaws close slowly on
the sky, and the head sinks back beneath the water.

Some scientists connect spy hopping with feeding. The vertical posture could bring heavier seafood to the bottom of a
whale's throat, where it is easier to swallow. To other scientists, spy hops are a form of male chauvinism. They occur re-
peatedly in one narrow neck of the lagoon where whales mate.
Here whale taps thunder and whale heads collide affectionately.
During this foreplay, the male's eight-foot penis emerges from
its recessed pocket. The courting pair then merge close to the
surface and begin revolving like a cumbersome lathe. Whales
are polygamous, and a high level of activity is maintained in the
mating area. A female in heat may be pursued by five males.

A year later, an impregnated female passes through Fornication Hole with a one-ton baby in its womb. The mother-to-be
cruises into more spacious waters called the Nursery. Gulls,
which congregate to feast on the afterbirth, indicate to human
observers when the underwater birth has occurred. In a fren-
zied cloud of white feathers, a new mother will lift its head clear
of the water. On top is the baby, some fifteen feet long. The

mother's head submerges and reemerges with the baby whale perched in the same place. The mother is teaching the newborn to breathe. Otherwise, two round-trip migrations, 24,000 miles in all, will go for naught. After a while, the calf will nestle close to its mother's underside, near the surface. The recessed nipples form an airtight connection with the calf's mouth that excludes saltwater. The calf does not suck; the mother squirts a gallon or two of milk down the calf's throat.

After six weeks, the mother leaves Scammon, trailed by the calf, which will be fully weaned in the microshrimp pastures of the Arctic Ocean. That trip will be the first of many migrations for this baby whale.

Other large whale species, on leaving the freezing polar seas in the fall, seek out more remote island sanctuaries—the Azores, Hawaii, Malagasy, Melanesia, New Zealand—as winter breeding grounds. Precisely because of its affinity for coastal lagoons, the gray reflects the whale's ability to survive human activity.

In the nineteenth century, Yankee whalers ventured into the open seas to track down the big blubber whales, following creatures faster and larger than their ships through icy gales, dead calms, and uncharted waters. In January 1846, a New England whaling ship en route to the polar grounds of the prized bowhead whale came to anchor in Magdalena Bay. The astonished crew saw countless whale spouts pricking through the calm blue waters. A whale-killing spree ensued. What was patronizingly dubbed the "mudhole season" came into being.

This patronization obscured a salient trait of lagoon whaling. On the open seas, a whale—once harpooned—tended to run and dive in the hope of shaking loose the whaleboat that clung fast to the end of the harpoon line. The shallow, confined nature of the lagoon thwarted this running tactic. The gray whale had to meet its tormentors head-on. More agile than the boats, the whale could change from the pursued to the pursuer. The harpooned gray would corner its tormentors and ram their wooden craft. Sometimes the gray's mighty flukes would clear the water and crash down on the luckless whaling crew in a

tactic called "lobtailing." Such cunning resulted in a bad press
and temporarily discouraged exploitation of the "devil fish."

In 1857, the brig *Boston* entered a previously ignored lagoon.
A jubilant captain, Charles Melville Scammon, could report,
"Two large cows were captured without difficulty, which gave
all hands confidence in our ultimate success." The next day,
before a whale could even by struck (harpooned), two of the
Boston's three whaling boats were staved in by flashing flukes.
Scammon found himself in command of "a crowded and contracted hospital. Our situation was both singular and trying.
The vessel lay in perfect security in smooth water; and the
objects of pursuit, which had been so anxiously sought, were
now in countless numbers about us."

One morning, a boat was lowered from the "crowded and
contracted hospital." The crew carefully hugged the shallow
lagoon shoreline, out of reach of the whales, and finally anchored inshore where the lagoon narrowed into Fornication
Hole. When a whale emerged to spout, a man in the boat shoul-
dered a new form of technology. The bomb-lance gun fired a
bomb lance that could pierce the whale's blubber and detonate
inside the whale's lungs. It had one drawback—a short range.
When the whale emerged again, the man aimed and fired. The
color of the whale's spout turned crimson. The man knew he
had successfully pressed the gun's range.

The following day, the whale was floating near the head of
the lagoon, buoyed up by gases decomposing in its blubbery hull.
Scammon was no longer in the business of pursuing whales. He
was ambushing them. The defiant grays had become as defenseless as steers in a stockyard.

Such bushwhacking quickly spread to other Baja lagoons.
Eleven whaling stations along the California coastline bush-
whacked grays en route to the lagoons. This commercial aggres-
sion could have but one end. By 1861, four years after Scammon
sailed into his namesake lagoon, gray whaling no longer paid.
Too few grays were left. An estimated 11,000 whales had gone
into the trying pots. This mortality did not include the nursing

calves that circled the ships where they had last seen their mothers. The whalers departed from the desert lagoons to find new grounds and to apply new techniques. From a prewhaling population of some 20,000 to 25,000, the grays descended to "no more than a few dozen," according to one San Diego naturalist in the 1930s.

In 1938, the International Convention for the Regulation of Whaling instituted a voluntary method of conservation quotas on whale kills. The convention, now administered by the International Whaling Commission, also accorded the gray a special status in recognition of its plundered condition: "It is forbidden to take or kill gray whales except when the meat and products of such whales are to be used exclusively for local consumption by the aborigines." Under this subsistence provision, an annual catch of about 180 grays from the western Pacific herd is conducted by a native tribe on the Soviet Union's Chukotski Peninsula.

With Scammon Lagoon off limits to whalers, the grays have brought their population level up to an estimated 20,000. But the beneficent clause of the International Convention protects them only from commercial exploitation. It does not protect their vital living space.

The Vizcaino Desert helps make central Baja California one of Mexico's least populated regions, but it does manage to host one small community. Guerrero Negro is surrounded by the source of its prosperity, giant solar salt ponds that stretch out of sight like snow-covered prairies. (The town's name is Spanish for "black warrior." According to legend, an eighteenth-century black pirate pounced on Spanish and British ships from this lagoon lair.) Those saline-rich waters of Scammon Lagoon which buoy up baby whales are pumped into these ponds daily. To up the annual salt production from one to five million tons, Exportadora de Sal, owner of the 300,000-acre salt concession, dredged part of the lagoon as a leading dock and a salt-barge channel. Barges transport the salt harvest to 100,000-ton tankers that cannot worm their way through submerged sandbars.

The tankers dock a hundred miles offshore in a deep-water harbor at Cedros Island. Much of the output goes to Japan. A Japanese firm, Mitsubishi, and the Mexican government operate Exportadora as a joint venture.

Although the 3,000 residents of Guerrero Negro, whose homes, shops, and gypsum roads are owned by Exportadora, are happy with such activity, some scientists who faithfully trek to Scammon Lagoon each January to document the gray's return from the "extinct and vanishing" category are less so. In 1960, Dr. Raymond Gilmore, conductor of a gray-whale census for the U.S. Fish and Wildlife Service, wrote, "The area available for calving and mating may be the most critical factor in determining eventual size of population. Reduction of this area by natural events or by man may have a pronounced effect in lowering the population ceiling."

Although barging activity at Scammon occurs in a lagoon arm not regularly frequented by the whales—a company decision based on engineering considerations, not conservation—there is no specified end to lagoon "development." With whale requirements at the mercy of industrial requirements, an eviction of whales from Scammon Lagoon becomes possible, either gradually or quite suddenly. Faced with a continuing takeover of its winter grounds in Baja, California, the gray would have to find new coastal breeding and feeding grounds, compete with other whale species for offshore grounds, or subsist on the open ocean. The uncertainty of such adaption intensifies scientific concern.

Such a prospect has a particularly galling significance to scientists. Just like commercial whalers, whale scientists must generally take to the open seas to track down the object of their professional curiosity. But observing a whale from a ship—if a whale is sighted—is like observing an iceberg: Most of what matters is not visible. As a result, even though factory ships know how to slaughter whales on an assembly-line basis, scientists know distressingly little about a creature that pumps blood through hundreds of feet of arteries at one pulse, maintains a body temperature of ninety-six degrees Fahrenheit in near-freezing waters, manufactures a mother's milk twice as rich as that of human mothers, and possesses a spongelike bone structure that can heal multifractures. Traditionally, many whale scientists have resorted to the study of slaughtered whales aboard whaling ships. As will be discussed later in this chapter, Japan justifies continued killing of endangered large whales on the basis of a need to continue such research.

The opportunity that Scammon Lagoon provides—a pondlike atmosphere in which to observe the world's largest mammal intimately—was first recognized by Captain Scammon, incredibly enough. While ordering harpooners to bomb whales, the self-educated Scammon was also measuring the girth of the victims, inspecting the contents of their stomachs, and executing precise drawings of their magnificent torsos. Like another whaling contemporary, Herman Melville, Scammon sensed that there was more to whales than oil to light cities and bone to corset cancan lines. In 1874, he made what the magazine *Science* soon declared was "the most important contribution to the life history of marine mammals ever published": *The Marine Mammals of the Northwestern Coast of North America.*

With the gray whale in the "almost extinct" category around the turn of the century, Scammon Lagoon slipped from scientific notice. In 1926, a Hollywood actor was cruising through the Baja lagoons in his yacht, *The Gypsy.* John Barrymore was entranced by two gray whales in "amorous dalliance . . . if anything so enviably and titanically active comes under the heading of dalliance." He whipped out his camera. "We eavesdropped, and I trust, for the stimulus of one's old age, recorded the largest mammals in flagrante delicto! A memorable day!" Barrymore, who harpooned a gassy rubber facsimile of a whale in *The Sea Beast,* then tried to accomplish the real thing on a gray but failed, according to biographer Gene Fowler.

Errol Flynn, a friend of Barrymore, was thrilled by these encounters. Shortly after World War II, the swashbuckling actor, son of an Australian biologist, personally chauffeured a

Scripps scientist to Scammon in his somewhat infamous yacht. Dr. Carl Hubbs, an ardent reader of Captain Scammon's life-work, confirmed that the gray whales existed in goodly numbers in the lagoon. This confirmation has since sparked eager scientific and tourist pilgrimages.

As a scientific whale observatory, Scammon Lagoon could become the place in which the whales could reveal their natural secrets to us. As a public whale observatory, it could become the place in which the gray whale could display its grandeur to the world. Already the gray is a major tourist attraction in southern California, an area in which the competition is fairly hectic. Each December, the National Park Service operates the world's pioneer whale observatory on strategic Point Loma. In addition, sport-fishing firms operate "whale-hunt" boats, whereby passengers pay just to see the backs and blows of whales. Yet 300 miles to the south, people can watch whales breach, spy hop, sleep, nurse, and mate, just from the shore.

As more roads and resorts penetrate Baja California's scenic remoteness, Scammon Lagoon could achieve its potential as a world-famous whale observatory—if carefully planned. Uncontrolled tourism could be just as harmful as unlimited industrial activity.

In 1971, Mexico formally designated both Scammon and nearby Guerrero Negro Lagoon as the world's first whale sanctuary. Contradicting the stereotype of a developing nation hell-bent on progress at all costs, Mexico was prepared to link bans on the killing of endangered whales to the need to protect their living space as well. Boating traffic is restricted during the calving season. When salt activities in Guerrero Negro Lagoon were shifted to more spacious Scammon, the whales returned to this forsaken calving ground. In 1979, Mexico designated San Ignacio Lagoon further south as its second whale sanctuary. Whale observation towers permit viewing from the shore.

In 1987, Mexico enlarged the Scammon Lagoon Sanctuary to include 7.2 million acres of surrounding desert and mountain areas. A research center is planned so that scientists can conduct permanent studies. While supportive of the reserve established by the Ministry of Urban Development and Ecology, Dr. Bernardo Villa of the National Autonomous University of Mexico wants "more strict vigilance. We lack the airplanes, helicopters, and boats to really protect the whales." Dr. Villa is also concerned by Exportadora plans for more expansion.

In 1990, a Japanese developer was proposing to build a billion-dollar mega-resort complex in Magdalena Bay, another major wintering ground for the gray. The complex would include its own international jetport, a golf course, a marina, and a seawater conversion plant. According to *Progresso,* a Mexican newsmagazine, the developer had one of his grandsons naturalized as a Mexican citizen to gain title to some 200,000 acres in and around the bay. Dr. Juan Guzman, a Mexican bird expert who lives in Baja, is urging the Mexican government to do environmental studies of the bay to identify potential impacts on the gray and on seabird colonies.

Coastal nations along the gray's migratory path are learning of the need to share in protecting the gray's living space. Gray whales, along with other protected and regulated marine species, have become entangled in huge drift gill nets a mile or more long off the California coast. In 1990, California voters approved a measure that phases out use of gill nets along the coast of Southern California.

Recently, observers reported that grays, in southern California waters, avoided nearshore migratory corridors. "We have received reports that grays, when approached, are more elusive," says Steven Swartz of the U.S. Marine Mammal Commission. Could the hectic development of the marine "frontier," from offshore oil patches to recreational armadas, eventually drive the gray away from the crowded nearshore, whose calmer waters provide rest stops for mothers and their calves on the return journey? Airplanes have buzzed grays; recreational boats have chased or cut across their paths; and some of the fun-loving folks on jet water skis have added to the aquatic bedlam. According to National Marine Fisheries Service (NMFS) guidelines to stop such hazing, boats are not to approach closer than a hundred yards, and airplanes are to stay 1,000 feet above. Further, boats are to run parallel to the whale's path and not across it. In 1989, the Orange County Marine Institute in Dana Point, California, gave a report on compliance with these federal guidelines. The results? One-fourth of the private boats observed by researchers approached *within* a hundred yards. Once, twenty-six boats converged on one startled whale that had to change its course and disrupt its marathon migration. Whale observation boats, by contrast, were generally found to comply with the guidelines because they are being paid to secure views of whales, not scare them away. The institute would like to obtain state support for a grant to educate private boaters on correct viewing etiquette.

Under certain circumstances, gray whales have approached observation boats in the Baja lagoons. Some are quite willing to be touched or stroked; others roll over to display their bellies and to be scratched by a broom. To Roger Payne, a senior scientist with the World Wildlife Fund, the "friendly whale phenomenon" is "the most interesting bond between humans and mammals I have seen." Payne is concerned that overly strict protective measures could discourage such encounters.

In 1986, after an extensive global campaign by environmental groups, the International Whaling Commission, over the objections of Japan, Norway, and Iceland, put in place a belated ban on commercial whaling of all large whales, including the blue, the humpback, the sperm, and the fin. (The ban may be too late for the blue: Its population has dwindled from a prewhaling 250,000 to less than 500.) The ban exempts whaling done ostensibly for scientific research. Despite protests from the commission, Japan killed 330 minke whales during the 1989–90 season by invoking this exemption. After giving their all for Japanese science, the select whales were rendered for their meat and sold commercially to fund more dead-whale research.

Contending that remote observation technology and whale sanctuaries like Scammon make dead-whale research passé, the administrator of NOAA in 1989, Dr. Willian Evans, noted, "There are some people trying to make this a whale-free world, and we would like to prevent that."

Taking a cue from the resurgent gray, environmental groups are stepping up efforts to protect the living space of all whales. The Dominican Republic has designated Silver Bank, a spawning ground for North Atlantic humpback whales, a marine sanctuary. In summer, the humpbacks migrate north to feeding grounds on Stellwagen Bank off Cape Cod. The Center for Marine Conservation and other environmental groups want to designate the Bank, a possible target for industrial mining, as a national marine sanctuary. A similar sanctuary has been proposed for the Pacific humpback off Maui, Hawaii. If the blue, despite its low numbers, can effectively reproduce and recover, its feeding grounds in the Antarctic must still be protected from careless boat traffic, oil spills, and krill overfishing.

Scientists like Dr. Robert Brownell, Jr., of the U.S. Fish and Wildlife Service are turning their attention to the "forgotten whales," the smaller cetaceans. Like the spinner and spotted porpoise caught in tuna nets, smaller cetaceans are particularly vulnerable to fishing nets.

The recovery of the gray creates its own unique dilemma. With the gray at or near its prewhaling population level, the question arises, Should the gray be "delisted" as an endangered or threatened species? Once delisted, whaling nations like Japan might seek to harvest the gray again. Because of the new economic and social benefits from observing live whales and because of environmental threats like pollution and habitat loss, environmental groups and some scientists are generally opposed to such delisting. But Dr. Brownell favors such a move as a means of focusing critical attention on species that are more endangered than the gray, such as small cetaceans like the Gulf of California harbor porpoise and great whales like the blue, bowhead, and right. Brownell contends that the gray, even if delisted, would still be protected by the Convention on International Trade in Endangered Species, which bans all trade in products derived from cetaceans, endangered or not. But Japan may have a different interpretation. Within U.S. waters, all cetaceans are supposed to be protected by the Marine Mammal Protection Act.

While their varied encounters with human activity become grist for political and policy debates, the gray whales continue to emerge from the quiet waters of Scammon Lagoon in gallant spy hops. They remind us of the formidable challenge to conserve cetaceans, both large and small, and the rewards therein.

CHAPTER FOUR

Second Chance for Wild Salmon

In 1978, the logged-out hillsides upstream from the world's tallest trees were hard to envision as national park land. They looked more like ground zero for a Hollywood nuclear epic. Landslides thundered down this battered section of California's rugged Coastal Range, ripping up whatever shrubs dared to regrow. Redwood Creek, once home to king salmon runs thick enough for farmers to pitchfork, was choked with mud. Yet that year Congress added 36,000 acres of this collapsing coastal watershed to Redwood National Park. It was a belated move to protect the salmon runs and the world-famous Tall Trees Grove, which includes a 600-year-old giant that rises to 367 feet and could shade out a football field.

A decade earlier, when the park was created in Humboldt County, "we tried to warn Congress that, to protect the redwoods and the salmon, you needed to protect the surrounding watershed," recalls Lucille Vinyard of Trinidad, who worked with the Sierra Club and other groups for the park. The boundaries drawn, however, reflected a political compromise among the lumber industry, conservationists, and budget-conscious federal officials. Only after the slopes had been logged and the ancient redwoods and salmon were threatened was more of the watershed acquired for protection. Congress then gave the Park Service the environmental equivalent of "Mission Impossible"— reclaim this devastated land before it destroys the very resources the park was meant to safeguard. The results of this ongoing effort reveal much about our emerging ability to restore key coastal processes and to regain a portion of our rich marine heritage.

The Redwood Creek watershed is modest in size but dramatic in character. The creek, only fifty-five miles long from its head-waters to the Pacific Ocean, drains about 280 square miles of land, most of it on the vertical. Steep slopes rise as high as 5,000 feet. The rugged watershed is the crunched-up product of two major tectonic plates—the North American Plate and the Pa-cific Plate—colliding head-on. The creek runs along the trace of a fault. Some seventy-four tributary streams tumble down and, in big rainfall years, turn the usually mild-looking stream into a raging torrent.

To many people, it was obvious that timber cuts on such a steep watershed would accelerate runoff and erosion. Before the advent of industrial logging, the coastal watersheds of northern California supported more than a half-million spawning salmon. Since then, salmon runs have declined by as much as 80 percent as their critical spawning habitat has been clogged by timber debris and mudslides. A major evolutionary asset of the salmon—the ability to spawn its orange eggs in freshwater sys-tems free of marine predators and to forage in the much richer food sources of the ocean—has become a liability. To protect just an isolated portion of a coastal watershed—whether it be a salmon spawning segment or a redwood grove—is to ignore how upstream activities can pervade an entire watershed.

The timber industry, however, was adamant. It was prepared to forsake control of the Tall Trees Grove, located on the allu-vial flats of a horseshoe bend, but not of the surrounding wa-tershed. With heavy machinery, the steep hillsides could be made to yield their redwood and fir stands. The state of California, with Ronald Reagan as governor, claimed that the mechanized harvests would be carefully regulated so that the industry would be a good neighbor. President Lyndon Johnson signed off on the original Redwood National Park bill, which included the Tall Trees Grove but excluded most of the basin. Later, one isolated redwood grove would be named after his wife.

During the next decade, families that staked their yearly vacation on a glimpse of the Tall Trees and the salmon spawning runs had to pass the gauntlet of logging trucks and stump-filled hillsides. One park overview was named Devastation Point. Going into the park was like going to Disneyland and getting the Texas Chain-Saw Massacre instead. Meanwhile, logging practices, some no longer allowed, served to unleash the slides and mudflows that intruded into the park. Slugs of silt raised the level of the Redwood creekbed by five feet, threatening to eventually flood out the Tall Trees Grove. "We knew these cutover acres would have to be restored if the park was to have a decent future," says Vinyard.

By 1978, Congress and the Carter administration, thanks in part to prodding by Congressman Phil Burton of San Francisco, wanted to redress this schizoid situation. The cutover acres were added to the park, along with $33 million in federal funds for reclamation. The timber industry, while in strategic retreat, still retained control over the upper two-thirds of Redwood Creek basin. California, now under the Jerry Brown administration, said the timber industry's hillside act would be cleaned up and that park officials could review timber harvest plans and inspect harvest sites in the upper basin. The redwoods and the salmon had ostensibly been saved . . . again.

No reclamation project of this scope had ever been attempted in an area of such dubious geology and steep terrain. The park's first plan of attack was a labor-intensive replanting program. A team of geologists, botanists, and rangers began to hike up the steep, slippery slopes, arms stretched out to keep their balance. "At first, a lot of time and labor was expended to replant barren slopes," explains park geologist Dave Steensen. Willow wattles, bundles of willow twigs, were buried on the bare slopes in the hope they would resprout and green up the hills. But this European technique proved time-consuming and not very effective on the drier slopes. Moreover, winter rains could quickly wash away such good intentions and carve out more deep gullies.

The team soon sensed they might be missing the forest for the trees. "We began to realize that old logging roads, not the cutover land per se, were a major culprit of erosion," says Steensen. Roads dammed up or diverted hillside streams, forcing winter flows onto barren, slide-prone slopes, creating highly erodible gullies.

The restoration team then shifted to a new tactic. It would stabilize or "put to bed" 300 miles of hard-packed haul roads and 3,000 miles of tractor trails. At the same time, it would also excavate and restore the original streambeds. "We couldn't do this with just hands and shovels," says Steensen. The Park Service enlisted an unusual ally. It hired some of the huge crawler tractors and hydraulic excavators that were building new logging roads in the upper basin to put old roads to bed in the park and restore streambeds.

Once a roadbed was "outsloped"—recontoured into the hillside—the plan called for its replanting with grass or trees to resist erosion. The healing team noticed, however, that this step might be unnecessary and even counterproductive. Bald spots along the retired roadbed were quickly colonized by coyote brush, salal, Douglas fir, redwood, and other members of the surviving forest community. This same community can reseed the barren slopes once the runaway stream flows are returned to their jilted beds. Plant grass and you would only slow the process of natural reseeding. Today, grass seed is out and straw mulch, up to 9,000 pounds per acre, is in. The straw protects the seedbed from sheet and rill erosion.

By 1983, such treatment forestalled erosion of some 6.6 million cubic feet of sediment—enough to fill up a 150-mile-long parade of dump trucks, according to park ranger Robert Belous.

Today, about half of the old road system has been put to bed and the greening continues. Even the view from infamous Devastation Point is green, from the light, bright shade of the new growth to the darker shades of taller, old, and advanced growth that can reseed the abused lands. You can believe you are in a National Park and not in a war zone.

Steensen and fellow geologist Darci Short took me to K and K Road, at one time a virtual industrial freeway that opened up so much of this ancient coastal forest to harvest. Foot by foot, mile by mile, this roadbed is being rolled up like a carpet, leaving behind a trail of decaying straw and thrusting green shoots. As the road goes, so goes easy access, whether for loggers, park car caravans, or fire-fighting units. This is a second-chance forest that is being put on its own again, free to confront lightning fires, slides, and droughts on its own evolutionary terms. When I return again, it will be on foot.

As we walked along a creekbed shaded by resurgent alders, we could see that another major resource is getting a new lease on life. As silt flows within the park boundaries recede, the waters of Redwood Creek can begin to clear. Remnant runs of salmon and steelhead trout can reclaim ancestral spawning grounds. The fish are receiving other assists. In summer 1989, Short supervised the removal of an old dam on Lost Man Creek, so salmon can regain more upstream habitat.

Historically, juvenile salmon drift downstream into Redwood Creek estuary, where they can feed and gain strength before leaving for the rich pastures of the Pacific Ocean. But flood-control dikes installed in the 1960s cut off flows to an arm of the estuary, South Slough, once used by salmon. Ergo, another restoration opportunity. "We installed a gated culvert in the dike to restore the flows," says park hydrologist Randy Klein. Flow levels can be controlled to prevent flooding of pastureland next to the slough. Today, with South Slough in circulation again, the estuary hosts up to 117,000 salmon a year, along with sea lions, sea otters, and flocks of pelicans.

Botanist Mary Hektner's restoration tools include a flamethrower and a small, gold-colored beetle. "The flamethrower destroys alien [introduced] weeds that choke off native wildflowers. The beetle chews up a toxic weed, the tansy ragwort, which can cause liver disease in grazing animals," explains Hektner. Another plant on Hektner's botanical hit list, pampas grass, has not been so easy to vanquish. "It is tenacious. We may have to use herbicides," she says. Some vanquished weeds could return to the park by hitchhiking on imported straw mulch. "We screen sources of straw to reduce this problem," Hektner states. "With local sources, we could wind up with the tansy ragwort again."

Today, the recovery process at the park attracts national and even global interest. Fishery and forestry experts from China, Norway, and Ecuador visit Redwood National Park to observe the restoration team at work. Closer to home, the return of green slopes and clear water has helped encourage community-based efforts to restore the Eel, the Mattole, the Inyo, and other battered watersheds along the northern California coast. Two former park geologists, Danny Hagans and William Weaver, are helping the U.S. Fish and Wildlife Service to restore two major salmon rivers, the Klamath and the Trinity. The California State Coastal Conservancy and commercial and sport fishing groups have supported such efforts. State Senator Barry Keene wants to create a permanent funding source for such efforts.

Traditionally, state and federal agencies have invested in fish hatcheries to make up for loss of salmon spawning habitat. "But hatcheries have never been able to offset the loss of habitat," says William Kier of the California Advisory Committee on Salmon and Steelhead Trout. Playing surrogate mother to salmon can be a costly and frustrating business. Hatchery-raised fish, reared in crowded pens for release into the wild, can be more prone to disease. They lack the genetic diversity of wild salmon runs. Each salmon creek, such as Redwood, has its own special salmon stock that returns to spawn in the parent creek. Scientists are now concerned that hatchery-raised fish, by interbreeding with wild stocks, could reduce stock vigor and diversity. "Natural, in-river spawning lowers the risks of such catastrophes. It improves chances for survival by distributing the fish throughout the spawning grounds and the time of spawning throughout the season. It assures there will be the diversity so critical to salmon survival through the ages," notes the California Salmon Commission.

Habitat restoration offers an economic benefit, too. Because of the loss of salmon spawning habitat and the shortfall from artificial salmon production, California, once salmon-rich, must import wild salmon from Alaska and Canada, pen-cultured salmon from Norway and Chile, and smoked salmon from Scotland. According to the California Salmon Commission, a state program to restore more Redwood Creeks could double current salmon stocks, adding $150 million a year to business revenues and generating 8,000 new jobs.

Besides demonstrating the potential for restoration, lessons being learned at Redwood Creek could help prevent other coastal watersheds from turning into geologic Frankenstein's monsters. The timber industry is now targeting the coastal watersheds of Alaska, this planet's last major staging grounds for wild salmon runs. "More careful siting and maintenance of hillside logging roads could avert future mudslides and more lost salmon runs," says geologist Danny Hagans. By requiring timber companies to keep road culverts clear of debris and unplugged, risk of stream diversions could be reduced. Dips at stream crossings could keep stream flows in their natural channels if culvert systems fail or become plugged. Careful geologic investigations can identify unstable hillsides where the risks of slides and massive silt loads could outweigh short-term benefits of lumbering. Based on their extensive investigations, geologists at Redwood National Park have been urging state regulators to consider such policies.

And with good reason. The upper Redwood Creek basin, which lies outside park boundaries, is currently being logged. "If road building is not carefully controlled, this area could become a loaded gun pointed at the park," says Hagans. In a rerun of the frenetic 1970s, the gains in controlling erosion within the park could simply be offset by activities upstream. Given the federal deficit, it is unlikely that Congress will step in again to buy up another cutover segment of the basin and undertake another round of reclamation.

What about state assurances that the Park Service would have a meaningful voice in reviewing upper basin harvest plans? "Beginning in early 1983, a change in administrative procedures implemented by the California Department of Forestry (CDF) effectively precluded National Park Service participation in the field review of timber harvesting and road construction plans on lands upstream of the Park Protection Zone but within the Redwood Creek Watershed," reads the Park Service's recent *Tenth Annual Report* on the status of Redwood National Park. According to the report, CDF allows park participation only if the timber company consents. "With rare exception, landowners regularly and routinely refuse access to park professionals for either pre- or post-harvest inspections," reads the report. In other words, the park professionals can inspect the consequences of harvesting—more sediment loads coming into the park—and little else.

As the Redwood National Park experience indicates, our emerging ability to restore coastal watersheds and wetlands can still remain hostage to upstream resource practices. Hillside tract developers generate damaging silt loads that set back efforts to restore salmon and steelhead habitats along the central and southern California coast. In Oregon as well as California, river flows vital to spawning salmon and to estuarine shellfish can be diverted to farm fields by water agencies. Federal water projects will deliver river water to farmers at subsidized water rates. The farmers, in turn, grow some crops, such as cotton, that receive federal price supports. Fish and fishermen have trouble competing against such a federal policy tilt. The NMFS, after declaring a winter run of salmon in the Sacramento River as endangered, is considering more such designations for salmon and steelhead runs all along the California and Oregon coast. In the Sacramento–San Joaquin Delta alone, a whole range of fish species—salmon, sturgeon, smelt, striped bass—shows serious signs of decline.

Across the continent, in Florida, careless watershed practices threaten another national park. Sugarcane growers dump dirty, nutrient-rich irrigation runoff into the fabled "river of grass" that sustains Everglades National Park. The nutrients trigger a major botanical revolution as native saw grass is being crowded out by dense stands of cattails. Coastal populations of wading birds have dropped by 80 percent. Shellfish stocks in Florida Bay that depend on a mix of fresh and salt water are in dramatic decline, too. "This park may become a wildlife cemetery," notes one park ranger. In 1991, the federal Department of Justice was pursuing a lawsuit against Florida for failing to protect the Everglades from such pollution. Ironically, another federal agency, the Department of Agriculture, provides federal price supports that keep the polluting cane growers in business and protect them from foreign competition.

Our coastal watersheds, however modest in size, play a vital role in sustaining some of our most valuable living marine resources, from salmon to sturgeon. Our emerging ability to restore vital spawning habitat within these watersheds provides us with another opportunity to reverse, not just slow down, the loss of our natural marine heritage. But this opportunity will be undercut if public policy still permits cane growers, loggers, tract developers, and water supply agencies to damage public resources with relative impunity.

PART TWO

Global Caretakers

CHAPTER FIVE

Boundaries for a Boundless Ocean

On one side of the invisible line, the cod is a fish worthy of abstinence by fishermen. Stray one inch to the east and the cod is fair game for the hooks and nets of Europe.

The cod is caught up in the age-old dilemma of trying to solve problems in the marine realm by relying on neat political boundaries. Canada's effort to restore cod stocks can be nullified once the cod stray beyond Canada's 200-mile-wide fishing zone. The oceans, because of their sheer extent and far-ranging processes, defy reliance on traditional political boundaries.

Some 500 years ago, nations were going to war over attempts to fence the marine realm. Out of this conflict came a grudging recognition that nations have more to gain by regarding the seas as a shared resource—a global commons—governed by a sense of mutual responsibility. Given today's renewed reliance on boundary setting, this conflict and its resolution are worth revisiting.

In the early sixteenth century, the concept of the high seas as a global commons, or *res communis* ("belonging to everybody"), was virtually nonexistent. The Baltic was divided up by Sweden, Poland, and Denmark. Ships sailing north of Bergen required a royal license from Norway, a region then under the Danish Crown. England regarded the North Sea as the "British Seas." Spain and Pòrtugal resolved to split much of the Atlantic and Pacific between them. In the papal bulls of 1493, the papacy approved of this monumental division.

These claims were not just illusions of grandeur. Pirates, particularly out of the Barbary Coast, were marauding. Coastal nations felt it was only fair to share the costs of suppressing raiders with users of the coastal seas. In keeping with their larger claim, Spain and Portugal also invoked the rights obtained by discovery and exploration.

From a national standpoint, the Iberian claim was a farsighted piece of statesmanship. It recognized how maritime technology could monopolize the trade, resources, and military advantages of the New World and the oceans between. In control of the oceans lay Iberian control of the world. Spain's galleons—sporting ample sail—carried wealth to outfit armies, artists, courtesans, and proselytizing monks.

As other nations improved their shipping, they realized just how farsighted the Iberian claims were and also how fiercely defended. When John Hawkins carried African slaves to Spanish America, his prospective customers raided his ships in the Caribbean. Though thousands of miles from Spain, Hawkins was still in Spanish waters.

The nations that accepted or bowed to the papal bulls of 1493 were, by the mid–sixteenth century, thoroughly disenchanted. Their ships, now using sail with greater facility than the galleons, nevertheless could not trade. Another occupation beckoned. The piracy so assiduously practiced by the Saracens became national policy for England, the Netherlands, and France. Privateering was conducted under a meticulous cloak of legality. Queen Elizabeth would hand out letters of reprisal that authorized Hawkins and his protégé, Francis Drake, to raid Spanish ships. Admiralty courts judged captured galleons— "prizes"—as good or bad. Few prizes were declared bad. The

Queen, the privateers, and the stockholders in the privateering vessels split the booty.

When Drake collected prizes while circumnavigating the globe, Philip II of Spain informed the queen that her English sea dog had no business being in *his* waters, much less freebooting there. The defiant queen knighted Drake and hung his navigation charts in her chambers. She then elevated the cause of privateering from national policy to a universal ideal: "The use of the air and sea is common to all; neither can any title to the ocean belong to any people or private man, forasmuch as neither nature nor regard of the public use permitteth any possession thereof."

Spain responded by launching the Armada. Some of the lumbering ships, half-oared, half-sailed, could ram and board enemy squadrons. England's full-sailed, more maneuverable fleet under Drake preferred to cannonade rather than ram. It also shot "fyreworks" into Spanish sails. The English victory heralded the advent of a truly national navy—able not only to repulse invaders but to set the front lines at the very shores of the enemy, however large its forces.

The defeat of the Armada did not serve to ratify the queen's concept of a common sea. It only created a power struggle for sea supremacy. Spain and Portugal did not back down on their exclusive claims. The enterprising Dutch were learning to trade, fish, and fight in a remarkable array of seagoing vessels. They cultivated a monopoly in spice and pepper and even began to corner the entire ocean hauling trade. Their herring fishery spent part of the year off the Scottish coast.

In Great Britain, subsequent rulers regressed from the queen's concept. Sovereignty was reaffirmed over the North Sea. The Dutch herring fleet was taxed to subsidize the country's uncompetitive fishery. To remedy another national shortcoming—too few sailors for the royal fleet—British captains boarded ships to draft British subjects and alleged deserters. The captain was sole judge as to who was a British subject; speaking English was not always a prerequisite. All ships in the

British Seas had to "vail bonnet" (strike the flag) in the presence
of English ships, even of royal yachts. Ships that did not do so
received a shot through the mainsail and a bill for the price of
the shot.

Amid all these lusty projections of national sovereignty, privateering was still considered "patriotic retaliation." The resulting anarchy troubled some people. In 1603, the Dutch were still
trying to horn in on the Portuguese monopoly of the East Indies
trade. The upset Portuguese had ambushed some Dutch ships
and murdered their crews. Admiral Jacob Heemskreck then
privateered the carrack *Catherine,* bound for Lisbon, in the
Straits of Malacca. A Dutch admiralty court adjudged the *Catherine* a good prize and distributed the proceeds to shareholders of
the budding East India Company. Some shareholders, including
Mennonites, refused their shares, claiming that privateering
was immoral. They threatened to form a new trading company
under French auspices. With its oceanic ambitions thus jeopardized, the Dutch government called on the state historiographer to justify privateering.

The historiographer happened to be an engaging young man
of twenty-one years. At eight, Hugo Grotius was penning Latin
verses by candlelight. At eleven, he graduated from the University of Leyden. At fourteen, he was drafting treatises on
astronomy and navigation and, at fifteen, earning a Doctor of
Laws degree at the University of Orleans. Grotius was a genius,
incapable of producing an ordinary patriotic tract. Instead of
defending privateering, Grotius set about to demolish the concept of exclusive use of the oceans. Queen Elizabeth's open-seas
policy was to undergo a process of scholarly review, refinement,
and amplification and come out as law. Began Grotius:

> The subject of our discussion is the Ocean, which was described
> in olden times as immense, infinite, the father of created things,
> and bounded only by the heavens; the Ocean, whose never-failing
> waters feed not only upon the springs and rivers and seas, ac-
> cording to the ancient belief, but upon the clouds, also, and in

certain measure upon the stars themselves; in fine, that Ocean which encompasses the terrestrial home of mankind with the ebb and flow of its tides, and which cannot be held nor enclosed, being itself the possessor rather than the possessed.

To buttress this last phrase, Grotius marshaled authoritative testimony. He quoted Cicero: "What is so common . . . as is the sea to those who be tossed by the waves, or the shore to castaways." He cited Plautus: "The sea's most certainly common to all." He even quoted the writings of a Spanish jurist, Vasquez: "In cases involving the sea or other waters, men do not and cannot possess any right other than that which relates to common use. . . . [S]ince navigation cannot prove injurious save perhaps to the navigator himself, it is fitting that the power and right to impede this certainly should be denied to all persons." Grotius also cited Vasquez's comment on his country's oceanic claim: an "absurdity."

After invoking precedents for an ocean that cannot be "possessed," Grotius proclaimed his own corollaries. On fishing: "The right of fishing ought everywhere to be exempt from tolls, least a servitude by imposed upon the sea, which is not susceptible of a servitude." On trade: "Anyone who abolishes this system of exchange, abolishes also the highly prized fellowship in which humanity is united."

Grotius then mocked the Portuguese for molesting ships that followed the natural law: "Are you indignant because we are acquiring a share in the winds and the sea? Pray, who hath promised you that you would always have these advantages?" Admiral Heemskreck was not only defending the East India Company: "The Dutch sailor knows that he is fighting in defense of the law of nations while his foes are fighting against the fellowship of mankind." Grotius entitled his brief *Mare Liberum* (*Free Sea*).

In place of exclusive claims and piratical retaliation, Grotius was offering the world a sea governed by a sense of mutual respect. But his treatise offended a world in which kings were regarded as a law unto themselves. *Mare Liberum* was rejected by Grotius's own people. He was swept up in a religious and political conflict peculiar to the times, imprisoned, and smuggled out of Holland in a trunk. As an adviser to France's Cardinal Richelieu, he expanded his concept of the laws of nations to cover diplomatic protocol, rights of prisoners of war, international law, and other policies relevant to a world community.

While its chief intellect prospered in exile, the Netherlands quashed the pacifist spirit in the East India Company. After shouldering aside the Portuguese, the Dutch established their own monopoly in the Indies and rebuffed British traders "for seeking a harvest at our expense, they escaping the cost."

Great Britain took even more direct steps to refute Grotius. His remark that "fishing ought everywhere to be exempt from tolls" especially rankled the Tudors. John Selden, celebrated in poetry by Ben Jonson, admired by Milton, and a benefactor of Hobbes, was commissioned to refute *Mare Liberum*. In his *Mare Clausum* (*Closed Sea*), the scholarly Selden observed, "There are a few, who following chiefly some of the ancient Caesarian lawyers, endeavor to affirm, or beyond reason to easily admit, that all seas are common to the universality of mankind." Selden invoked his authorities for a private sea. He even cited King Canute's order to the tides not to touch the royal hem.

During the seventeenth century, the British and the Dutch engaged in hot and cold wars over "striking the flag" and an attempt to rejuvenate the British fishery through the pockets of Dutch fishermen. Patriotic piracy continued to disrupt the rising merchant order. Amid such ocean anarchy, Grotius's concepts, offering the prospect of armistice, became more attractive. They also made possible a different type of possession. A sea common to all would reward those nations that could best exploit its resources, whether to fish, trade, or project naval power. The British began paying less attention to sea salutes and impressment and more attention to improving the merchant marine, the high-seas fishing fleet, and conditions in the Royal Navy. A Scottish surgeon, Dr. James Lind, founder of nautical medicine, cured one impediment to naval recruitment—scurvy—with lemon juice. To save His Majesty's fleet from another disabler—tiny marine borers—shipbuilders sheathed hulls in copper. Captain Cook surveyed the resources of the Pacific. A century later, Darwin became acquainted with kelp aboard the HMS *Beagle*. The British were becoming oceanographers as well as mariners.

In the eighteenth and nineteenth centuries, this national effort came to fruition. The Royal Navy bound an empire together. "The ships of English swarm like flies, their printed calicoes cover the whole earth and by the side of their swords the blades of Damascus are blades of grass," cried out a furious pasha. The English merchant and fishing fleets dominated maritime trade. To maintain this global reach, the British Foreign Office popularized mare liberum.

The rest of the world was, by this time, willing to accept a common ocean. Although Britain enjoyed dominance, other nations might still pursue their own maritime aspirations. The Ligurian, the Adriatic, the Baltic, the North, the Atlantic, and the Pacific emerged from servitude, free of both tolls and privateering. Grotius's law of the sea was most persuasive. It did not have to be ratified by a constitutional convention and encouraged reciprocity rather than retaliation. The self-regulating machinery of the shared-use concept—plenty of room for trading vessels and fishermen—could be set in motion. The Golden Rule at last became practicable.

One form of sea sovereignty did survive, however. Developing nations, sensitive about their independence, felt the need to secure their coastal waters from smuggling, impressment, neutrality violations, and other possible projections of sea power. Grotius himself admitted to such a qualification. But how wide should a territorial sea be? Suggestions varied from twenty miles, or as far as the eye could see, to the range of coastal cannon, approximately three miles. One young nation, liberated from

British control but not British sea dominance, decided to set a specific boundary. In 1793, Thomas Jefferson, secretary of state for the United States, chose the more modest cannonball standard.

The evolving law of the sea rose not from one national claim but from its acknowledgment by other nations. Less powerful nations responded favorably. Even England adopted a three-mile limit around its island. A narrow—but not necessarily three-mile—territorial sea became accepted maritime law. (Thomas Fulton, in his book *Sovereignty of the Seas,* noted that Jefferson later devised another territorial sea. In 1807, he told France's Genet that our national jurisdiction extended "to the Gulf Stream, which was a natural boundary." His 1793 boundary proved to be longer lasting.)

In the same gradual and peaceful manner, as shipping increased, merchant navies began to draw up "rules of the road." So-called contiguous zones became recognized in customs, national security, and other carefully defined areas of national interest. At the same time, nations refrained from broad claims of sovereignty. In 1918, in responding to a letter from a citizen who said he had discovered oil forty miles out in the Gulf of Mexico, the U.S. State Department said, "The United States has no jurisdiction over the ocean bottom of the Gulf of Mexico beyond the territorial waters adjacent to the coast."

The common-sea concept, embraced by Queen Elizabeth and refined by Grotius, would win the praise of twentieth-century law scholars. In *The Public Order of the Oceans,* Professor Myres McDougal and William Burke have observed, "The outcomes of inclusive, cooperative enjoyment—as several centuries have demonstrated—can be genuinely integrative, with all winning and none losing, in a tremendous production and wide sharing of benefits."

Today, the concept of a global commons can seem quaint and antiquated as nations expand their borders seaward to enclose oil fields and fishing grounds. Grotius's assertion that fish stocks should be open to all comers was based on the belief that fish were inexhaustible. Today, our technology has made this premise obsolete; however, relying on boundaries to settle marine problems can reopen many of the same issues that split apart nations 500 years ago. Grotius's belief that laws for the sea should transcend national claims can become more relevant than ever.

CHAPTER SIX

The Wandering Tuna: In Search of Stewards

The Eastern Tropical Pacific (ETP) extends 2,000 miles out from the western coast of Central and South America. This ocean is the alive ocean, flaunting its fertility like the green parrot jungles of Central America. Flocks of seabirds are as common as clouds. Whales blow and seals bark. A porpoise does not merely show its fin. It can vault clear of the ocean, all the time revolving in the air. The spinner porpoise can do this in unison with a thousand of its kind. The ocean suddenly resembles a stadium in which an army of gymnasts perform somersaults on cue.

Such fertility attracts an all-star cast of swift predators. One hunter moves in schools as thick as buffalo herds, as swift as squadrons of waterfowl. The yellowfin tuna can range a thousand miles and more, sound more than eighty fathoms, and attain speeds of forty miles an hour.

This superb hunter is itself prey. In the global competition for sea food, the yellowfin is a prime target. This competition has become so relentless that the marine ecosystem itself is at risk. Nations that have pursued the tuna with a vengeance now wonder whether they can join together to avert such environmental boomerangs.

The yellowfin tuna ranks in the aristocracy of fishdom. Most coastal fish are dun-colored, to blend with the seafloor. The yellowfin sports the beautiful camouflage of the high seas, a metallic blue top and a silvery underside, all fine-scaled. The blue foils detection from above, the silver from below. The fins and a stripe along the body give off a yellow glow that suggests a tuna may semaphore by flashing its body.

Yellowfins can spawn at all times of the year. The eggs hatch in forty-eight hours, and within a year the larvae can grow into seven-pound fish. Tuna larvae are prized by small fish and adult tuna. Their mortality rate, according to biologist Witold Klawe of the Inter-American Tropical Tuna Commission, runs close to 100 percent. To compensate for this astronomic mortality, a tuna can spawn up to eight million eggs at one time. An egg that manages to survive will weigh 150 pounds by its fourth birthday.

To evade sharks and to sustain its swift growth, the yellowfin requires exceptional speed, range, and depth-sounding capabilities. Its fins symbolize this mobility. Whereas the stubby and webbed fins of coastal fish resemble a whisk broom, those of the yellowfin are long and lean. Its pectorals span out like wings to brake or stabilize underwater flight. The tail fin is an arc—a sweeping scimitar. Setting this simple screw in motion is a deep-bodied torso of concentric muscle. The flesh is not white but pinkish, colored by tremendous amounts of oxygen-giving blood that powers high-seas foraging. (The temperature of most fish equals that of the water; the spirited tuna is generally ten degrees centigrade warmer than its environment.) The yellowfin forages after squid, flying fish, swimming crabs, octopuses, and the general abundance of the ETP. Marine biologist Franklin Alverson, who classifies the yellowfin diet as "rather cosmopolitan," has found wood, kelp, feathers, and "unidentified material" in their indulgent stomachs.

A great fishery requires an abundant stock, and the rapid

growth and turnover of the yellowfin meets this requirement. The fish must also be nutritious and appealing. The protein content of tuna matches that of red meat without the accompanying fat calories. It contains iodine to prevent goiter, fluorine to thwart tooth decay, phosphorus to build bone, and vitamin B_{12} to enrich red blood cells. The yellowfin exemplifies the nutritious richness of the ocean, a richness many food authorities see as one key to our survival on a congested planet.

Under the freedom-of-the-high-seas concept developed by Grotius, tuna and other highly migratory fish, such as swordfish, were considered common property, available to all individuals and all nations in need of their value. But this availability can be restricted by another factor, the ability to catch and distribute such fast-moving, wide-ranging fish. Up until the mid-1950s, the U.S. tuna fleet relied on laborious pole fishing to catch tuna one by one in the rich ETP grounds.

In 1956, the clipper *Anthony M.* set out after tuna, but when the mast man cried "Boil," no bait was chummed, no ramps unhinged, and no poles grabbed. On reaching the boil, the clipper, proceeding at full speed, launched a power skiff off the stern. The two-man skiff and the clipper sped off in opposite directions and then started closing toward each other in a giant circle. When they met, a fat mound of nylon netting was spooled into the ocean to form a wall of webbing some 200 feet deep and more than a half-mile in diameter. The only exit for tuna lay downward, but a winch on the clipper swiftly drew this exit shut like a purse string. A power boom contracted the massive circle into a bag. Power-driven dip nets brailed the thrashing tuna into brine tanks, as some crew members tried to disentangle porpoises.

Pure seining had finally caught up with the tropical tuna. Although five pole fishermen were required to land one hundred-pound yellowfin, the Puretic power block atop the boom could reel in a hundred tons of netted tuna. The whine of gears replaced the grunts of labor. In 1960, the Alive Ocean yielded a record 234 million pounds of yellowfin.

Meanwhile, the Japanese were running out of tuna in the Western Pacific. The Indian Ocean proved rich in tuna stocks, but, again, long-lining thinned them out. Tuna cruised in the Atlantic, but apparently not in great numbers. Accordingly, Japanese long-lining vessels began fishing the ETP. Soon they were dropping fifty million hooks a year—hooks that snared marlin, sailfish, big-eye tuna, and the prized yellowfin. The competition was becoming more intense—Canadian fishermen made their debut—but the ETP was still prepared to fill more nets, more brine tanks, and more mouths.

The freedom-of-the-high-seas concept permitted these industrial nations to send their fleets into the ETP and hunt the tuna within three miles of the coast of Latin America. Three nations—Chile, Peru, and Ecuador—responded by asserting fishery jurisdiction 200 miles out on the basis of conserving the tuna stocks.

As others had done before, the three nations invoked conservation to serve a less selfless purpose. The tuna clippers with their jaunty lookout masts, the huge seines hanging from the power boom like magnificent filigree, the brine tanks stuffed with yellowfin hard as logs—all these offshore sights were galling reminders of the "economic inequality of the states," as one Latin American diplomat explained. That these clippers could pluck yellowfin within three miles of their shore and transport the catch 5,000 miles away seemed unjust. The freedom-of-the-high-seas concept was one not to be cherished but to be wary of, a potential lever to widen even further the gap between the haves and have-nots, a means by which industrial nations might usurp the resources of the adjacent sea.

By the early 1970s, the United States was under pressure to adopt the same type of galloping sea sovereignty. Upset by the presence of factory fishing fleets from Japan and Europe, coastal fishermen in New England and the Pacific Northwest urged that the United States extend its fishery jurisdiction 200 miles seaward. A schizophrenic quality began to overtake the nation's traditional allegiance to a spacious high seas. In a get-tough policy with "blackmailing" Latin American nations, Congressman Tom Pelly (R.–Wash.) urged the U.S. Navy "to send a gunboat down into those waters and protect our fishermen." At the same time, this fishing warrior, sensitive to complaints of fishermen in his home state over the presence of Japanese and Soviet fishing fleets, urged that the United States extend its sovereignty over the waters of the continental shelf—up to 400 miles wide in some places.

Another policy controversy was brewing. In 1966, a young scientist joined the U.S. tuna fleet to study how and why dolphins associated with schools of yellowfin, a bonding limited to the ETP. A concerned William Perrin (now with the NMFS) saw how a single net set on tuna could drown more than 1,000 dolphins, unable to escape the encircling wall of webbing. Such repeated "incidental kills" jeopardized the stocks of two dolphin species—the spinner and the spotted. The ETP dramatized another problem created by mechanized fishing technology—incidental capture of nontarget species. As environmental groups began mounting boycotts against tuna products, Congress passed the Marine Mammal Protection Act in 1972, requiring the U.S. tuna fleet to reduce its dolphin kill. While reducing its kill rate, the U.S. tuna fleet complained that foreign fleets were not obligated to do the same.

Nations that disagreed about solutions to such transnational policy snarls did agree on one point: The traditional law of the sea needed to be revised to reflect the proliferating problems created by technology and the increased marine expectations of both developed and developing nations. In 1973, the third United Nations–sponsored Law of the Sea Conference convened. After a decade of negotiations, the conference produced the 1983 Law of the Sea Convention. The convention would codify the right of each coastal state to establish a 200-mile-wide Exclusive Economic Zone (EEZ) in the adjacent sea. Here the coastal nation would exercise fishery jurisdiction. The claim by Chile, Ecuador, and Peru, once so controversial, had finally prevailed.

The convention must be ratified by sixty nations to come into force. As will be discussed in the next chapter, other provisions in the convention make ratification by key industrial nations questionable. Most coastal nations, however, including the United States, have unilaterally adopted the EEZ.

In accepting the 200-mile-wide zone, the world community has based control of much of the living resources of the sea on a geographical quirk. Those nations with the most ocean front-age have become the biggest winners. As it turns out, of the top ten winners, six happen to be industrial nations: the United States, Australia, New Zealand, Canada, the Soviet Union, and Japan. (The other four are Brazil, Mexico, Indochina, and Chile.)

While permitting a select group of nations to exercise control over a large portion of the world's marine protein supply, the world community has obtained very little in the way of mean-ingful standards to ensure wise conservation. Moreover, the convention places tuna and other highly migratory species in a political no-man's-land. As before, tuna continue to transcend political boundaries, however spacious, with impunity. Recog-nizing this troublesome mobility, the convention does encourage coastal nations to participate in regional forums to manage trans-boundary stocks.

Thanks to the foresight of the United States and a group of Central American nations, there has been such a regional forum in the ETP since 1948. The Inter-American Tropical Tuna Commission (IATTC) was established to conduct research on tuna and recommend conservation regulations *before* stocks be-came overfished. In 1966, an annual quota for the yellowfin tuna was established. Once this quota was reached, the fleets were to stop fishing. By adhering to this quota, the United States and other major tuna fleets conserved the yellowfin stocks while tuna stocks elsewhere were under stress from uncon-trolled fishing.

Nonetheless, this sort of transnational cooperation has been overtaken by the competition to corner the tuna catch. Mexico has decided to withdraw from the IATTC for the time being. With this defection, catch quotas to protect yellowfin have been curtailed. Mexico prefers a commission comprised only of those Latin American nations which border the ETP; nations wanting to fish in the ETP beyond the 200-mile national limit would need a permit from this proposed commission. To the United States, Canada, and Japan, this seems like a very arbitrary approach to tuna management. The approach remains in the formative stage; the smaller Central American nations fear domination by Mexico. (Panama has already seized those tuna clippers from Mexico that intruded into Panama's EEZ.)

With the U.S. tuna fleet's access to fishing grounds jeopardized by EEZ after EEZ, Mexico has added to its development debt to enlarge its tuna fleet. Today, Mexico catches more ETP tuna than the U.S. fleet, which has shrunk to half its 1972 size. Yet just like the Yankee fishermen, the Mexican tuna fishermen find that technical proficiency can be undercut by political boomerangs. Mexico wants to export its tuna to the world's largest consumer of canned tuna, the United States. But the United States has placed periodic embargoes on tuna from Mexico. The Marine Mammal Protection Act requires those nations wanting to export tuna to the United States to adopt regulations that reduce porpoise kills. In 1990, U.S. canners adopted a policy of buying only tuna that is caught with "dolphin-free" technology. The ability of Mexico to comply with these strictures remains to be seen. Environmental groups want independent, on-board observers on each tuna vessel that fishes in the ETP.

The shrinking U.S. tuna fleet has shifted to dolphin-free tuna grounds in the South Pacific, seemingly beyond the reach of extended sea sovereignty. But sixteen island nations with names like Kiribati, Tuvalu, and Vanuatu complained that the U.S. clippers were invading their combined EEZs. This claim was not opportunistic. For these tiny nations, inshore tuna catches can constitute the GNP and have great social and cultural import. When the Soviets offered to recognize the island EEZs and buy fishing permits, another U.S. institution became involved in tuna diplomacy. The Defense Department does not want a Soviet foothold in the South Pacific, *glasnost* or not. So the U.S. State Department decided to strike a bargain with Vanuatu and company. In 1987, the U.S. tuna fleet received a five-year general permit from the island nations to fish in the waters of the southwestern Pacific; in return, the island nations will receive $60 million in U.S. development aid. This sudden unity did not extend to establishing a regional commission able to monitor tuna abundance. As a result, the relentless competition to catch tuna engulfs the entire Pacific Basin.

This competition has generated the most destructive type of catch technology. Japan, South Korea, and Taiwan have deployed drift gill nets up to thirty miles long in the South Pacific. While ostensibly targeting squid, these nets can catch tuna, swordfish, and other more profitable fish species. Indeed, Australia and New Zealand have attributed a decline in tuna catches to the wide deployment of these nets. These "walls of death" can also trap thousands of seabirds and dolphins. Based on protests by the United States and the nations of the South Pacific, the United Nations in 1989 passed a resolution to ban high-seas drift netting by 1992 unless protective measures could stop the by-catch slaughter. This resolution will test the ability of nations to support and enforce measures to protect the marine ecosystem from destructive fishing practices. There are reports of Asian drift net fleets moving into the Atlantic, where bluefin tuna and swordfish stocks are already being overfished.

Today, 60 percent of the world's tuna catch comes from the Pacific Ocean, with yellowfin still a major market catch. During the 1990s, the global seafood industry is counting on an accelerated catch of tuna throughout the world oceans to make up for sharp declines in cod and other groundfish stocks. According to James Joseph, the current IATTC director, however, most tuna species are at or near full exploitation, except for skipjack. As the international competition to expand market share and pay off development debts intensifies, the tuna will be fished harder and harder. If the catch decreases and tuna prices rise, the hunt will become even more frenetic. If this fishing frenzy extends to forage-fish stocks, the stressed tuna stocks will have that much less food available. Eventually, the hunt will cool down. Whether it does so because the stocks are depleted or because disparate nations like the United States, Mexico, Japan, and Vanuatu accept the challenge of managing the nomads of the sea remains to be seen.

While this challenge, given such varying national interests, seems formidable, some recent scientific and technical developments may help. The range of highly migratory fish can frustrate adequate monitoring and enforcement of fishing regulations. Based on multinational treaties, salmon on the high seas are supposed to be caught only by the country of origin— the country with the salmon spawning watersheds. For decades, U.S. officials have suspected that some Asian fishing fleets, including squid drift netters, have been illegally catching salmon in the North Pacific. In August 1990, the U.S. Coast Guard found 12.5 tons of illegal salmon in the freezer holds of a Japanese vessel in the North Pacific. The presence of the vessel outside a squid fishing boundary had been detected by a satellite monitoring system the NMFS deploys to assist in apprehending such violators. Such a satellite monitoring system could help enforce the United Nations resolution on high-seas drift netting in the South Pacific. (It could also serve to detect potential illegal high-seas dumping of toxic wastes and oily ship discharges or spills.)

Why porpoises and tuna bond together in the ETP, thus making the porpoise so vulnerable to netting, remains a scientific mystery. Yellowfin tuna, however, do not always swim with porpoises. Sometimes tuna aggregate around driftwood or drift seaweed, where they can be netted without catching porpoises. The NMFS has experimented with Fish Aggregation Devices (FADs) to build on this dolphin-free catching opportunity. IATTC scientist Witold Klawe has proposed a program by which driftwood would be deployed throughout the ETP and then tracked to see where yellowfin were most likely to converge on the planted driftwood.

By undertaking such projects on a joint basis, nations can evolve a sense of shared responsibility toward sustaining the living oceans. The plight of the tuna and of seabirds trapped in nets in the middle of the ocean reiterates the urgent need for such a vision.

CHAPTER SEVEN

Staking Out the Deep Seabed

Thousands of miles from the nearest continent and three miles below the surface of the Pacific Ocean lies a stretch of seabed that would seem to be well beyond the influence of national governments. Yet in these deep ocean depths some six nations, including the United States, have staked out expansive claims to a lumpy rock that resembles a baked potato.

The rock is a manganese nodule. Its presence on the ocean floor has incited visions of a marine mineral rush while disrupting conferences on the evolving law of the sea. Such turmoil is normally associated with gold, silver, and other precious metals. The nodule stirs controversy without sustaining even a single commercial mine. How can this rock inspire such expansive visions and global ill will?

The first large oceanographic expedition, that of Britain's HMS *Challenger* in 1873–76, retrieved the first nodules. Scientists disagreed over whether the potatolike lumps came from submarine volcanoes or as "gifts from outer space."

The nodules, thought to contain only one commercial mineral, manganese, emerged from obscurity in the 1960s. After conducting research at Scripps Institution of Oceanography, Dr. John Mero wrote *The Mineral Resources of the Sea* in 1965. Mero, through laboratory analyses, stressed that the nodules contained not one but four commercial metals: manganese (used to strengthen steel), copper, nickel, and cobalt. As Mero wrote, "We have, in the ocean, materials that are available without removing any overburden, without the use of explosives. . . . [T]here will be no drifts to drive, shafts to sink, or townsites to construct in developing a deep-sea mine." Are these deposits located in fog-bound, cold waters such as the polar seas? The most promising deposits occur in the tropical Pacific between Hawaii and Central America. For miners accustomed to jungles and snow-covered mountains, a more comfortable era of mining appeared to beckon.

Could there possibly be more good news? Unlike fish and timber, mineral deposits are not renewable. That is why miners, whether from ancient Greece or today's world, must locate new sources. Metals found in the nodules precipitate from the seawater. They collect around a core that may be a shark's tooth or a squid's beak. Nodules are being formed through this process even now. Minerals that grow! What more could miners ask for?

There appeared to be one problem. Nodules occur in deep water beyond the continental shelf, "deep" being on the order of two, three, and four miles. One skeptic likened recovery to "trying to pick up peas with a straw from the top of the Empire State Building—at night." But initial field tests indicated that nodules could be sucked up by vacuum pipes or retrieved via a chain of buckets. The location also appeared to be a political plus. Deep-sea miners would operate far beyond crowded coastal waters, seemingly beyond the reach of governments, tax demands, and requirements for union crews. Mero, however, suggested one possible caveat: "that of fomenting inane squabbles over who owns which areas of the ocean floor and who is to collect the protection money from the mining companies."

In 1966, during the launching of an oceanographic research

vessel, President Lyndon Johnson observed that we should not "allow the prospects of rich harvests and mineral wealth to create a new form of colonial competition among the maritime nations. We must be careful to avoid a race to grab and hold the lands under the high seas. We must ensure that the deep seas and the ocean bottoms are, and remain, the legacy of all human beings." This vision was meant to discourage national seaward claims that might control or limit mining access to the nodules.

A year later, Malta's ambassador to the United Nations, Arvid Pardo, turned this solemn presidential announcement around in a manner that shook up the expectant miners. To Pardo, phrases like "legacy of all human beings" meant that the international community, instead of safeguarding access for corporate miners, should control exploitation. Most developing nations immediately embraced Pardo's concept that the nodules on the deep seabed were part of the "common heritage of mankind."

Miners once worried about national claims were now confronted by the specter of an international claim to every single nodule in those tantalizing underwater photos. But one American institution was not so dismayed by Pardo's reformulation of the ocean commons. The Defense Department was concerned that developing nations, eager to reject their colonial pasts, would limit transit through strategic straits and coastal waters. The U.S. delegation to the United Nations, encouraged by the Defense Department, decided to favor international control over the deep seabed as an incentive for developing nations to maintain transit rights. In 1970, the United Nations General Assembly, by a nearly unanimous vote, declared that the resources of the sea beyond national jurisdiction are "the common heritage of mankind."

Seabed mining, once a poor political cousin to fishing, navigation, marine oil development, and marine pollution, suddenly became a prime catalyst for the Third United Nations Conference on the Law of the Sea (LOS), which began in 1973. Given the initial optimistic projections of nodule wealth, there appeared to be room to compromise on an international seabed authority to protect claims of miners while sharing a portion of royalties with the world community.

To American miners, the political advantages of the nodules began to recede. After locating seabed deposits and developing recovery technology, a miner's return on this investment might be determined by an amorphous body of "international do-gooders, bleeding hearts, and political pipsqueaks" inclined to cream off the revenues from such private risk taking. The specter of public controls became acceptable to the American mining community . . . if administered by the United States. (The head of one mineral exploratory venture working the waters between Hawaii and the United States referred to this stretch as "the American Ocean.")

To developing nations, such arguments only buttressed their fears of a seabed grab. In the LOS sessions, the developing nations, banding together as the Group of 77, proposed an international seabed authority. This authority would exclude private mineral leases and do the mining itself; revenues would go into a global fund for developing nations. To American miners and their congressional supporters, this position served to prove that developing nations wanted to make seabed mining a keystone for a new international economic order.

The fate of world fisheries tended to harden the position of the Group of 77. At the behest of Latin America, most developing nations promoted the concept of a 200-mile-wide Exclusive Economic Zone (EEZ) off each coastal nation. In effect, the coastal waters, where fish stocks are most abundant and easily harvested, would be controlled by coastal nations, depending on the length of their coastlines. The biggest winners turned out to be industrial nations in the Northern Hemisphere, including the United States, with its two-ocean coastline, and Denmark, which controls the largest island in the world, Greenland. With so much of the living marine resources beyond the reach of the new international economic order, the fate of the deep-sea nodules took on added import. Projections of their potential wealth seemed to rise. If the Group of 77 could not land more fish, why not try for the potatolike lumps in the ocean depths?

The United States at first withheld support of a 200-mile zone as leverage to get the developing nations to accept a seabed authority with only limited powers. When Congress, under pressure from U.S. domestic fishermen, went ahead and unilaterally adopted a 200-mile zone, the leverage—whatever its value—vanished.

In 1983, the conference finally produced a broad-ranging Law of the Sea (LOS) Convention that protected navigation rights. The 1983 convention included a seabed mining regime acceptable to most national delegations—but, as we will see shortly, with some significant holdouts. An International Seabed Authority would control deep-sea mining. Private corporations, national ventures, and the authority itself could mine. How could the authority, without any real capital or equipment, expect to mine? A private or national contractor would be required to submit two prospective mine sites. One site and the appropriate mining technology would be transferred to the Enterprise, which would mine for the authority. Each contractor would be required to make the technology available to the Enterprise "on fair and reasonable commercial terms" and, under certain conditions, to some coastal developing nations. The Enterprise first would have to make good-faith efforts to obtain technology on the open market.

The authority would set production ceilings on each lease so that land producers would not be unduly affected. The authority could compensate land producers that "suffer[ed] serious adverse effects" from seabed mining. Lease royalties would go toward such payments. The major commercial nodule mineral is nickel, the recovery of which could generate manganese far beyond market demand. If sold or dumped on the world market, this manganese could undercut the economies of Zaire and Zambia, current producers of manganese and cobalt.

With such broad powers, the authority could tilt in favor of mixed mining efforts or predominantly Enterprise efforts. The Enterprise could seek bank loans and would be exempt from any taxes. Incentives would be provided for nations or corporations to gain mining access through joint ventures with the Enterprise.

Who was to control the authority? The convention tried to spread voting control among three groups—developing nations, Western industrial nations, and the socialist nations of Eastern Europe. The hope was that no one group would dominate; the fear was that two groups would form an alliance. To counter this latter option, a unique voting formula was created. A three-tier system would divide up policy decisions by differing voting majorities. Major leasing issues would require a consensus, defined as the absence of a formal objection by any member state; less momentous matters would be decided by two-thirds or three-fourth votes.

All parties to the LOS convention would be obligated to lend interest-free capital, based on a scale of assessments for the regular United Nations budget, to fund the Enterprise's first mining project. The funding level was set at $1 billion, of which the U.S. share would be about $250 million, depending on how many nations ratified the convention.

Given the expectations of seabed wealth and the tensions between industrial and developing nations, the mining regime in the LOS convention—while cumbersome—represents considerable progress. The national delegations to the LOS conference voted overwhelmingly to adopt the convention, including the mining regime. Some 130 delegations voted yes, 17 abstained, and 4 voted no. While the 1980 U.S. LOS delegation felt the regime represented a reasonable compromise, the 1981 delegation appointed by the incoming Reagan administration echoed concerns of American miners over the "giveaway" of the deep-sea nodules. The United States cast one of the four "no" votes, primarily because of the proposed mining regime. The mining regime was also of concern to a group of European nations that abstained from voting—West Germany, the United Kingdom, the Netherlands, and Belgium. The Soviets abstained, too.

The overwhelming approval of the convention by the conference delegations has no legal force. To come into force, the convention must be ratified by sixty nations. Even if the convention comes into force, nonratifiers like the United States could undercut its effectiveness. (By 1990, some forty-three nations had ratified the convention.) Without the United States and major European nations contributing to the financial support of the mining regime, the regime will be off to a rocky start. The United States, the United Kingdom, Japan, France, Italy, and West Germany have enacted unilateral mining laws designed to recognize seabed claims by their nationals. In 1987, these nations, along with Belgium, the Soviet Union, and Canada, entered into "reciprocating state" agreements to eliminate competing claims and claim overlaps.

By 1989, the United States had granted four firms exploration licenses involving some 496,651 square kilometers of seabed within the Clarion-Clipperton Fracture Zone in the east-central Pacific Ocean. France, Japan, the Soviet Union, Germany, and the United Kingdom have granted licenses in this zone, too. Germany has also granted a license in the deep seabed south of the Galapagos Islands. The exploration licenses granted by the United States last for ten years. The license holder can apply for a commercial recovery permit during this period.

After giving lip service to the deep seabed as the "common heritage of mankind," the United States and its mining allies have started to divide up huge amounts of the seabed in the east-central Pacific. Where this process will end no one really knows. Will other Pacific Rim nations like Australia, China, and Mexico remain passive, or will they enter the mining claims sweepstakes? Will this process be extended to deep subsea deposits of oil, an activity that could reach economic maturity well before nodule mining? What recourse will the global community have against seabed miners that, despite environmental assurances, wind up contaminating marine resources, including tuna and other open-sea fish stocks?

The potential environmental impacts from deep-sea mining reiterate the need for a greater global perspective. Initially, such impacts were thought to be negligible. Mining would occur on the deep seabed, where life is supposedly limited by the extreme depths. In the past decade, however, scientists, armed with remote television units, have detected a surprising abundance of more than 400 species at these deep depths. A constant rain of sediment and detritus from the upper ocean layers provides nutrients for bottom-dwelling fish and clams. These bottom forms, in turn, play a role in recycling the nutrients and making them available to the marine food chain. One fish, the rattail, feeds at deep depths and becomes prey for fish in the upper water column.

Regardless of whether the nodules are scrapped or sucked up from the ocean floor by mining technology, the bottom, or benthic, species would undoubtedly suffer heavy mortality. Recovery would be slow because these bottom dwellers tend to have a very low reproductive rate. Even bottom dwellers beyond the mining sites could be affected. The mining would generate clouds of sediment that could suffocate seabed communities hundreds of miles away. According to Clifton Curtis, a U.S. environmental lawyer active in LOS issues, a 1,000-ton-a-day nodule mining project could stir up more than 4,000 tons of sediment.

As the nodules are brought up to the mining ship, surface sediment plumes may be formed. These plumes could restrict light penetration and reduce the plankton growth that sustains fish higher in the food chain. The Clarion-Clipperton Fracture Zone, the current target of mining claims, overlaps the migratory route of the yellowfin tuna and other highly migratory fish in the mid-Pacific. In an age of expanded marine exploitation, no marine area, even in midocean, enjoys isolation from wideranging industrial impacts.

The United States and its mining allies claim that such impacts can be controlled, although a 1990 United Nations report on the marine environment warns against such confidence. Yet given the sheer extent of the mining claims and the presence of commercial tuna stocks, such assessments should be subject to independent review. The LOS convention was one step in this direction, but its future is now in doubt.

To Elliot Richardson, a former head of the U.S. delegation to the LOS conference, the U.S. rejection of the landmark LOS convention could eventually jeopardize LOS provisions for navigation rights that U.S. maritime and naval interests consider so vital. As the United States and its mining allies stake out the deep seabed, other nations may decide to pick and choose what LOS provisions suit them. As in the case of tuna and other highly migratory fish species, the temptation to compete for marine resources—real or illusory—can prevail over the search for cooperation.

Fortunately, there may be an opportunity to reassess the issue of seabed mining before it turns into a political and environmental time bomb. Even with a mining regime, national or international, little or no seabed mining is expected to take place for some time. In a 1989 report to Congress, the National Oceanic and Atmospheric Agency (NOAA), which administers the Deep Seabed Hard Mineral Resources Act, noted, "The presently depressed level of world metal markets has dimmed prospects for commercial mining in the near term."

Meanwhile, the projected costs to mine can spiral. Equipment must be more durable than research equipment that makes a few seabed grabs and returns to an onshore marine laboratory. The equipment must withstand water pressures of 6,000 to 9,000 pounds per square inch, saltwater corrosion, and near-freezing temperatures. It can take twenty to sixty minutes to get one nodule from the seabed to the ship. (A slurry method may shorten this time.) This vertical distance can severely complicate a ship's ability to relocate on a particular site. Imagine that from a helicopter you had to extract gravel with a two-mile-long pipe as the link. You would have to hover through wind gusts and clouds while changing the length of the pipe string as the terrain below changed from hills to valleys. You would have one advantage over the marine miner—you could at least eyeball the land below.

The miles of pipe required to reach the seabed creates a large weight suspended from the ship. The pipe string itself stretches under this weight, like a spring under tension. The relationship of the suspended pipe to the ship becomes somewhat analogous to that of a drawn arrow to a bow. If part of the pipe snaps off, the remainder may spring back and pierce the ship's hull. Currents in the water column or a nodule collector snagged on the seabed can snap the pipe.

Another overlooked factor: Ore deposits—even when high grade—can be expensive to process. To separate various metals from the host rock can be very costly. Rocks rich in silica pose such problems, and nodules are rich in silica. Solve separation and you can contend with another problem: the large amounts of energy needed to fuel processing. According to nodule researchers with Kennecott Copper Corporation, the cost to process nodules will be nearly double the cost to recover them.

A major environmental and social problem posed by marine mining involves the need for onshore processing sites. Hilo, Hawaii, once agog over the idea of becoming the world's seabed mining capital, now wonders whether a processing facility would pollute the environment and compete for scarce energy resources. The facility would produce copious tailings containing arsenic and other toxic elements. The municipal host will have to share shrinking space in its existing coastal dump sites, obtain new sites, or both. If dumped in coastal waters, the wastes may pose risks to marine life and to recreation. "Who wants to be the Pittsburgh of the tropical ocean?" asks one Hilo resident.

Even if a mining firm finds a tolerant community and learns to separate metals from silica-rich nodules, it may have to compete with firms processing silica-rich ore deposits mined on land. In other words, metal sources on land promise to outcompete marine sources for some time. Formation of minerals on land benefit from one advantage that the marine environment lacks: weathering.

(In the late 1970s, scientists researching active seabed rift zones where the continental plates are spreading sighted thermal vents, or chimneys. The vents eject polymetallic sulfides that can contain zinc, copper, lead, and silver. Ergo, another marine mineral rush. Excited officials with the U.S. Department of the Interior found that one active rift zone existed within the nation's EEZ, seemingly beyond the future reach of a global seabed authority. In the early 1980s, Interior Department officials invited miners to bid on leases on the Gorda Ridge some 170 miles west of the California-Oregon shore. The silence was deafening. The lease proposal has been shelved. A NOAA survey reported no active vents on the ridge and therefore no production of polymetallic sulfides. A 1987 report by the National Academy of Sciences on hard mineral resources in the U.S. EEZ classified polymetallic sulfides as a "speculative resource.")

In hindsight, a more careful assessment of the technical and economic aspects of seabed mining might have helped to prevent it from subverting the spirit of the LOS convention. With this realization, the opportunity to get the convention process back on track arises. As developing nations realize they cannot expect a windfall from deep-sea mining and as industrial nations recognize the need for a stable marine regime, the mining issue could be revisited with much less heat, perhaps in a special session of the Preparatory Commission established by the United Nations to deal with LOS convention matters. The developing nations may be willing to accept a larger role for private firms in the International Seabed Authority as long as some of the benefits of this enlarged access accrue to the global community and firm environmental safeguards are developed. At the same time, more urgent issues, such as transnational pollution, high-seas drift nets, and an accelerated rise in sea level could be

addressed with a renewed sense of shared responsibility. As
Grotius pointed out more than four centuries ago, to treat the
ocean as a global commons is to respect its universal character.
To permit an illusive marine mineral rush to distract us from
this idea is to invite folly.

CHAPTER EIGHT

Blinders for the Ocean

The year is 1995. A U.S. vessel is anchored off a coral reef that fringes the southern tip of India. An Indian naval destroyer, siren sounding, comes alongside. Armed sailors board the U.S. vessel, place the ship's captain under guard, and direct the ship to the nearest Indian port.

Is the U.S. vessel suspected of smuggling drugs, dumping toxic wastes, or catching scarce shrimp? No. This vessel contains scientists racing against time to ascertain whether rising sea levels threaten to gradually drown the shorelines of the world. The global community's need for such critical research, however, can become subordinate to one nation's right to control the comings and goings of marine scientists. Like tuna and whales, marine scientists can become prominent if unwitting victims of seaward nationalism.

Most of what we know about the sea has been learned only in this century. The pioneer oceanographers were as bold and innovative as the marine explorers and artists who preceded them. Sir John Murray served on the first oceanographic expedition, the *Challenger* expedition sponsored by Great Britain in

1872. For lab space, he would remove cannons from the naval ship. To retrieve seabed samples, he would arm a hand lead used in soundings with sticky lard or tallow. One sounding could take two hours; one dredge sample, an entire day. The sail-powered *Challenger* took more than three years to cover 68,000 miles while probing the world's oceans. Much of the equipment was left snagged on the seabed. Of the 243 members of the crew, 61 deserted. There were two drownings, one suicide, one accidental poisoning, and ten cases of syphilis. It took nineteen more years to publish the *Challenger's* fifty-volume report. This was a pretty fair output of work considering that there were only six scientists on board. Their sampling work eventually resulted in the discovery of 4,714 new species.

Always short of funds and equipment, the pioneer oceanographers learned to share human and financial resources without regard to nationality. To identify thousands of *Challenger* geologic and biological samples, British scientists recruited German, Norwegian, French, and U.S. scientists. The British press was upset by the use of "foreign naturalists," but one British scientist, Charles Darwin, defended this practice.

Today, our technical ability to research and understand marine processes has expanded manyfold, but our ability to deploy this technology collides with political barriers that would astound the pioneer oceanographers. Under Grotius's concept of the freedom of the high seas, marine scientists had an open passport to study the marine environment. While their counterparts on land often had to secure permission from suspicious farmers to explore, the Murrays did not worry about this matter: There were no trespassers on the oceans. Today, though, it is unlikely that the *Challenger* expedition could be effectively repeated. Its mobility would be subject to the approval of dozens of nations. The coastal zone off the continents is where key ocean currents occur and where up to 90 percent of the biological activity occurs. Here atmosphere and ocean interact and shape our climate. Here most of the world's undersea earthquakes occur. Here many of the answers concerning the history of the earth are to be found. Here, too, the human impact on the ocean is most intense. But in today's world, a marine scientist can find access to such a key area cut off.

As nations extended their borders seaward in the 1970s, many marine scientists assumed they would be exempt from controls. They thought of themselves as seeking knowledge about the ocean, not exploiting it. This knowledge enables coastal nations to benefit from marine resources. To U.S. legal scholar William Burke, freedom of scientific access "is the primacy upon which progress can be made in conquering and preserving the ocean environment for the shared benefit of all people." As a sign of good faith, marine scientists reiterated their willingness to notify coastal nations of research cruises ahead of time ("prior notification").

But coastal developing nations tend to see no difference between marine research and the ultimate exploitation of their resources. As one Brazilian diplomat observed in a United Nations debate, "In the last analysis, every particle of scientific knowledge could be translated into terms of economic gain or national security. In a technological society, scientific knowledge means power." Indeed, marine scientists in the United States continually reaffirm how pure research eventually pays off. Even the appearance of research technology belies any clearcut distinctions. Equipment in geophysical research, such as seismic survey and drilling equipment, resembles oil exploration gear. When the *Pueblo* was seized off North Korea, the U.S. Navy described it as an "environmental research ship." As if such semantics were not enough to make coastal officials suspicious, marine scientists must take repeated measurements to monitor marine processes. To coastal officials, such monitoring appears to put their coastal waters under constant surveillance.

Marine scientists often assure coastal officials that there will be "open publication" of results from coastal surveys. Ironically, this assurance can backfire. Historically, discovery of a mineral deposit in a developing nation can unleash political power struggles, sometimes financed by foreign interests seeking lucrative exploitation leases. The last thing a coastal nation wants is "open publication" of a possible new offshore oil deposit, an underutilized fish stock, or an outfall that pollutes regional waters.

Many coastal nations thus assert a very broad control over marine scientific access in the 200-mile-wide Exclusive Economic Zone (EEZ). This concept is referred to as "prior consent." Despite objections from the scientific community, this concept prevailed in the Law of the Sea Treaty.

Let's say you must organize an oceanographic expedition. The principal research area will be off Brazil, but you plan to conduct research all along the South American coast. To start, the State Department's Research Vessel Clearance Office sends you a standard form. You must name all the researchers and technicians and enclose their curricula vitae. Next you must outline your proposed route, your field stations, and when you will be at these stations. (What happens if you cannot maintain this schedule because of sea storms or mechanical failures? You'll ask for clarification later.)

Next you must declare that ship space will be reserved for observers and researchers from the host nation. You call the State Department. How much space is enough? The more space available, the more likely permission will be granted. (You begin to revise upward your budget estimates for food.)

You must provide a copy of all the information the expedition obtains. This can mean providing plankton samples and seabed grabs, as well as computer readouts of temperature and salinity.

You must secure permission from each nation whose coastal waters you pass through, regardless of how short a period of time is involved. And nations often have differing requirements. Colombia, for example, requested that 30 percent of the cost of one expedition in its coastal waters be paid to specified Colombian institutions. The expedition sponsor, Scripps Institution of Oceanography, decided to go elsewhere.

Some nations may insist on prior approval of publication of

your research. Most if not all scientists will bypass coastal waters rather than submit to such a condition.

The response to your application comes in due time. It is yes, but with a condition: If you delay or change the schedule, you must apply for prior consent again. This sort of repeat consent makes a mockery of scientific opportunity. A scientist who comes across a significant finding, such as an accelerated sea level rise on a reef off India, wants to take more measurements. But the time to do this will violate his permit, and a new request may require another six months of processing time. He might risk doing this anyway, and, as in the example at the beginning of the chapter, face detention. And waiting for six months for a permit to study a rapid-response event—a coastal earthquake or a transnational oil spill—is another way to hobble marine knowledge.

To what degree is marine research actually being inhibited by the need for prior consent from countless coastal nations? Since 1986, up to 20 percent of the research clearances the U.S. State Department forwards on to coastal nations have run into problems. Some nations have denied permission outright or requested more information. Some have attached unacceptable conditions. Recently Mexico has tried to charge $500 for approving a research clearance. This charge is ostensibly for administrative processing; the most popular destination for U.S. research cruises is Mexico. The biggest problem, however, has been late approvals. The research vessel has simply had to drop its plans to visit one coastal zone in order to maintain its schedule. It can cost up to $14,000 per day to operate a research vessel with a twenty-two-member crew. Waiting around for late approvals—and late guest participants—can be costly. In 1989, the U.S. research vessel *Endeavor* was held up for two days while awaiting arrival of a Brazilian naval officer. This wait required a revision in the research proposal, which was then denied by Brazil. "The LOS Treaty problems facing marine scientists may be even more complex than the research they are trying to perform," observes Dr. David Ross, a marine policy expert at Woods Hole Oceanographic Institution.

Canada and most European nations are more cooperative in providing coastal access. The Soviet Union, which once severely limited scientific access, has been encouraging U.S. research vessels to visit its coastal waters. Marine geologist George Keller of Oregon State University didn't even have to retain a U.S. research vessel to explore China's continental shelf; he was invited to go along with a Chinese research vessel. The United States, like Norway and some other European nations, requires prior notification only from those foreign research vessels which want to enter the 200-mile-wide EEZ.

Ironically, the scientists most affected by restrictions on marine science access are in the nations that originally campaigned for the prior-consent concept. Scientists in Latin American nations, often short of equipment and research funds, are eager to collaborate with foreign scientists. Yet as one Brazilian oceanographer once observed, "a wave of stupid nationalism considers collaboration in science almost like the crime of 'collaboration' in war." India, to the consternation of its marine science community, rarely approves any research requests by foreigners. "In a way, we are being cut off from the rest of the world community," one Indian researcher has noted.

Ostensibly, prior consent could provide coastal nations with the clout to impose conditions on visiting expeditions, that is, special research tracks to aid local researches. In theory, prior consent could then be used to instigate a transfer of technology. Approximately 75 to 90 percent of the world's ocean research capability—the critical mass of scientists, ships, and instruments—resides with six nations: the United States, the Soviet Union, the United Kingdom, Germany, Canada, and Japan. Some European states possess more of a regional capability: Norway, Sweden, Denmark, France, Spain, Portugal, Italy, and Poland. Thus, six nations have the power to carry out most major marine research projects.

Nevertheless, the most critical scientific need for developing nations may not be temporary space on board a research vessel or access to endless computer printouts of salinity levels. Such nations need equipment for their own onshore labs and coastal vessels. Their students need access to foreign universities for specialized marine training. In short, they need to develop their own technical and human resources onshore. For scientists in the United States and Europe, a strengthened marine community in the Third World means an expanded ability to monitor global trends in sea-level rise, marine weather, biological stocks, and pollution.

To develop such scientific links, Scripps Institution of Oceanography (SIO) in La Jolla, California, has established the Interamericas Program. According to Dr. George Hemingway of SIO, research vessels helped distribute some 68,000 technical journals and other printed materials at ports near Latin American research institutes. Through the program, Mexico and the United States have resumed cooperative research projects on the California current, including assessment of transboundary fish stocks like sardine and anchovy. Upward of thirty-six Mexican scientists have participated each year in SIO cruises. The University of Southern California (USC) has entered into a student and faculty exchange program with two universities in Mexico's fast-growing Baja California region. "Through this program, USC has been able to extend its coverage of regional earthquake activity 800 miles south by sharing data with Mexican scientists. This saves us thousands of dollars in research funds," explains Dr. Robert Douglas, USC's dean of natural sciences. Pro Esteros, a joint U.S.–Mexican organization, monitors migratory bird counts along the Pacific Flyway and promotes protection of coastal wetlands. Dr. David Ross, a marine policy expert at Woods Hole Oceanographic Institution in Massachusetts, has urged the United States to create an Office of International Marine Science Cooperation to serve as a focal point for foreign contacts seeking to develop cooperative programs with the U.S. marine scientific community and vice versa.

Original acceptance of the prior-consent concept was undoubtedly influenced by the fact that coastal nations were trying to protect their natural resources from uncontrolled exploration. Ten years ago, the marine frontier was still being regarded as a resource bonanza. Today, more critical needs have emerged—the need to understand, predict, and restore key environmental processes from the status of fish stocks to global climate change. To inhibit marine science access is a blind blow for continued marine illiteracy on a watery planet. Cooperative marine programs, it is hoped, will help restore an open-ended passport for marine scientists around the world. Given a better sense of trust between industrial and developing nations, prior consent might be phased out. In a world growing anxious about the advent of rising sea levels and sinking shores, we cannot afford to place marine science at the mercy of a hundred separate permit officers competing to set conditions—and fees—on research at their own leisure.

A diver glides through a sea forest of kelp off Canada's Vancouver Island. If protected from pollution and overharvesting, seaweeds promise to be an important part of our marine future.

National policies that favor more oil production can make coastal regions hostage to more oil spills. To reduce the risk of black shores, coastal regions must shift to less polluting energy sources.

Our ability to catch fishes can exceed our ability and willingness to replenish their stocks. In the future, nations that rebuild such stocks and restore fish habitats will gain a vital advantage over nations that, because of apathy, wind up with too many fishermen and not enough fish.

From the United States to the Soviet Union, the damming of river basins cuts off fresh water critical to coastal and marine ecosystems. A shift to more efficient water use would help restore salmon runs, oyster beds, wetlands, and eroding deltas.

While the natural shore is resilient enough to absorb the pounding of coastal storms, the "immobile" urban shore, because it must meet storm waves head on, is sometimes more vulnerable.

Another coastal ecosystem, the barrier island (such as South Padre Island, Texas, pictured here), is being lost to runaway coastal development that defies dangers inherent in predictable hurricanes. Government disaster aid, however, is recruited to make up for this policy oversight.

Deltas are becoming an endangered coastal ecosystem. Here, cypress forests in the Louisiana delta region die as salt water intrudes along navigation canals.

The use of the coastal environment as a cheap dump has left a legacy of closed oyster beds, restricted beaches, and seafood health advisories. As developing nations rush to industrialize, more living marine resources will be lost to this wasteful policy.

Debris litters another shoreline, this one on the island of Aruba in the Caribbean. We can expect more trashed shores if we fail to reduce and recycle our soaring wasteloads.

Hurricanes can turn fishing boats and floating debris into dangerous battering rams. If coastal development continues to overtake tropical shores, a boat like this could ram a condo rather than a tree.

PART THREE

Our Coasts,
Our Future

CHAPTER NINE

The Drowning of the Sandy Shore

Recently I visited a southern California beach of my boyhood. The sun was shining, the waves were up, and the sea sparkled. But the beach was gone. In it place was a foot-bruising strand of rocky cobbles. I was looking at what may be in store for the American shore.

Shoreside development eager for a front-row seat on the coastal action can devastate our magnificent coastlines. The barrier islands and sandbars of the Atlantic Coast; the dazzling white beaches of Florida that tinkle as you walk on myriad shells; the sparkling, cliff-backed sands of California; the coral and black volcanic shores of Hawaii—all are at risk.

The risk extends beyond the loss of favorite sun-in-the-fun showplaces. A beach is more than the ocean's welcome mat. It is a geologic bumper, absorbing the attack of waves and currents that would otherwise chew away coastal land. As this geologic bumper erodes, our coastal regions find themselves on a collision course with high tides and hurricanes. In 1989, Hurricane Hugo slammed into South Carolina, racking up a mind-numbing $6 billion in property damage. To avoid more punishing collisions, we must reform public policies that can subsidize risky development.

How can our desire to enjoy the shore destroy it? Imperfect understanding of the dynamics of sea and beach is one reason. Beaches are lively landforms that survive by retreating and advancing in concert with the ocean. Yet people blithely build their dream homes in "active" beach zones. Some builders actually bulldoze view-blocking dunes, an action comparable to knocking down a river levee. Dunes serve as natural storm-surge barriers and provide beaches with a sand reserve. When they go, it isn't long before waves collide head-on with dream homes, as happened during Hurricane Hugo. And when large-scale development imposes immobility on a shoreline, as it has in such cities as Miami, Tampa, and high-rolling Atlantic City, large-scale disaster is courted.

Much of the Atlantic and Gulf coasts are rimmed by barrier islands, low-lying strips of beach and dune separated from the mainland by elongated bays, or sounds. In its natural state, a barrier island can retreat, or "roll over," in response to storm surges and tidal incursions, ensuring its continued existence and protecting the mainland shore. But when development deprives it of that resilience, the barrier island has no bumper to cushion the ocean's force. The resulting impact can be as violent as an auto colliding with a trailer truck and just as lethal.

Even communities that keep a respectful distance from active beach zones can be thrust by shortsighted neighbors into punishing collisions with the ocean. Beaches are nourished by sand carried in currents running along the shore. In California, this "sand river" is fed by coastal watersheds that drain quartz-rich mountain ranges. Eroding coastal bluffs supply the material to build up Cape Cod beaches. Offshore sandbars help sustain the barrier beaches that rim the Gulf and Atlantic coasts. Coral reefs and lava fields help sustain Hawaii's sparkling white and black beaches. On both our Pacific and Atlantic coasts, the predominant direction of this sand river is north to south, so

that sand from Georgia beaches, for example, helps sustain
Florida beaches.

When this vital sand flow is impeded, downcoast beaches can
drown. Assateague National Seashore in Maryland may wind up
as an underwater park. Upcoast of that seashore, in Ocean
City, Maryland, a harbor jetty extends out into the sand river.
The jetty traps the sand that once sustained the Assateague
shore. The Atlantic advances as the sand-starved shore retreats,
sometimes at the rate of fifty feet a year.

Dams can also trap the vital flow of shore-sustaining sand
grains. In southern California, Los Angeles beaches can shrink
as inland dams trap some fifty-two million cubic yards of sand.

Such predicaments generate pressure for federal action to
"stabilize" America's disaster-prone shore. At first, the Army
Corps of Engineers, a federal agency involved in coastal protection, adopted a fortification approach, building concrete seawalls and rocky groins to hold beaches more or less in place.
Hawaii's Waikiki Beach is cluttered with forty-two groins and
thirty-seven seawalls. A seawall's steep face, however, can foster a severe backwash that undermines whatever beach remains.
Seawalls are now considered a major cause of the erosion that
plagues Waikiki Beach. Moreover, the waves that undermine a
beach may eventually undermine a seawall.

Sea Bright, New Jersey, residents live in the shadow of a
towering, prisonlike seawall spray painted with graffiti. "If you
remove the seawall and let nature take its course, Sea Bright
will disappear," says Duke University geologist Orrin Pilkey.
"The beach wants to be hundreds of feet behind where the
seawall is." The seawall is fronted by the rubble of its prede-
cessors. The shore, steepened by rising wave action, can no
longer hold sand. The seawall itself is beginning to slide seaward; storm waves periodically overtop it.

A groin juts out from shore to trap sand for a starving beach.
If an upcoast jetty or inland dam is already impounding the sand
transport system, a groin is of no more help than a fork to a

starving man. If there is still sand to stop, the groin will do the job—for the upcoast beach. The beach downcoast will erode that much faster. Downcoast property owners may erect groins to compete for what sand grains remain. Today, more than 300 groins in various stages of storm-battered decay protrude fang-like from the New Jersey shore. From the air, the shore resembles a steeplechase run. (Some groins can shunt sand out to deeper water beyond the reach of the beach zone and the long-shore current.)

The Army Corps of Engineers now prefers to pour sand onto beaches rather than concrete into seawalls. But this nourishment approach is not without problems. A beach denied its natural sand supply must be nourished again and again. In southern California, Surfside–Sunset Beach, starved by an upcoast jetty, is on its sixth synthetic beach. Waikiki has imported sand from thirty miles away; some sand-short hotels manufacture their own sand by crushing coral. In the hectic struggle to feed beaches, the Army Corps even mines offshore sand deposits with mixed success. Some deposits have been contaminated by dumped chemicals. A more convenient source—sand bypassed from sand-trapping harbors—can suffer from the same toxic residues.

The artificial-nourishment approach poses a special problem for the barrier islands of the Atlantic Coast. Here sea level is rising a foot or more each century. This may not sound substantial until you realize the low-lying nature of the barrier islands, particularly if the dunes have been bulldozed. A one-foot rise in the sea level could extend storm surges 500 feet and more inland. To attempt to stabilize an urban barrier island with a seawall or a new beach is to expose it to a greater frequency of punishing storm surges. The shore itself may become too steep to hold imported sand. Original or synthetic dunes may be undercut and toppled by the rising sea levels.

When you play sandman to a stressed shore, you need a deep pocket. The Army Corps restored Miami Beach at a cost of $7 million a mile. ("Freeways are cheaper to build," one official has noted.) In 1991, the Army Corps of Engineers was involved in a program to rebuild Sea Bright's seawall and to pump in twenty-three million cubic yards of sand to form another synthetic beach. The cost to protect the 1,800 residents: $250 million. "The most comprehensive approach to this," notes New Jersey state coastal official John Weingart, "would have been to move all the buildings away and say this is not a safe place to live." The Miami Beaches and Sea Brights, with federal help, can afford such costly sand fixes. Communities without political clout cannot, and they remain geologic invalids.

Ironically, the federal government can encourage the very storm-prone development that lobbies for federal sand fixes. Federal grants have been available to help water, pave, bridge, and otherwise urbanize hurricane-prone sand mounds. Under the National Flood Insurance Program, the federal government even insures at subsidized rates properties in coastal high-hazard areas against storm damage. Home owners can submit damage claims storm tide after storm tide. Repeat claims, which involve about 2 percent of total insured properties, account for 43 percent of the total losses from the National Flood Insurance Program. The Federal Emergency Management Agency has identified some 30,000 properties as in the "repetitive-loss" category, many in coastal high-hazard areas. In 1990, John Knauss, administrator of the National Oceanographic and Atmospheric Administration, told Congress that some $60 billion worth of coastal property is covered by federal flood insurance, making it the third largest liability of the federal government after social security and the savings and loan debacle.

Once hit by predictable disasters, coastal regions can apply for federal disaster relief to rebuild for a return engagement. South Carolina has received some $2 billion in federal disaster relief in the wake of Hugo. While such relief is vital to getting communities back on their collective feet, too often it can make up for sloppy land use and building controls. According to a postdisaster survey by federal officials, many homes left roofless by Hugo were built in violation of wind design standards. Such costly oversights are supposed to be caught by local building inspectors. But these inspections can become cursory as coastal towns undergo building binges.

Alabama's Dauphin Island has been able to rely on federal disaster twice in the past decade to rebuild hurricane-prone structures. Ironically, its growth has been induced by a federal disaster grant to rebuild a bridge wiped out by Hurricane Frederic in 1979. Cost: $39 million. Number of full-time island residents then: 1,600. Federal subsidy per resident: $24,375. Island ferry service would be cheaper than a bridge and less vulnerable to the next hurricane, but that option was overlooked with Uncle Sam picking up the tab and realtors subdividing more sand lots.

Before long, we may count the price of runaway shore development in lives as well as money and property. After a hurricane surged through Galveston, Texas, in 1900 and left 6,000 dead in this barrier island city, the United States began developing an elaborate hurricane evacuation system. Thus, while Hurricane Hugo racked up $6 billion in property damage, only twenty people died. Some 264,500 residents heeded hurricane warnings and retreated inland.

This system, however, is being pressed to the breaking point by the sheer intensity of coastal development. One mishap—an auto collision, a bridge closed for repair—could trap thousands of evacuees. According to the National Hurricane Center, the New Jersey coast; the Norfolk, Virginia, region; the Florida Keys; and the Florida west coast are most vulnerable in terms of coastal population having exceeded hurricane evacuation facilities. "This nation is more vulnerable to hurricanes than it has ever been," says hurricane expert Neil Frank. Porter Goss of Florida's Sanibel Island told a congressional subcommittee, "I'm scared to death if we have a hurricane whether or not we are going to be able to save all the lives that we are supposed to save on that island." Sanibel's average elevation is six feet, well below the twenty-foot-high hurricane surges that could sweep across the island. Up to 15,000 people flock to this prized sand strip; one auto accident on the bridge to the mainland could paralyze evacuation and trap thousands, possibly as night falls. Broadcast warnings could be drowned out by honking horns, fender benders, overheated radiators, and rising winds.

Thousands more would have to be evacuated in the Miami, Florida, area come a major hurricane. The city of Miami can no longer depend on its natural storm barrier; Miami Beach has been rendered immobile and vulnerable to storm breaches by its development binge. Even with twelve daylight hours' warning time and buses for senior citizens and hospital patients, state and local officials worry whether bridges and highways could handle a massive evacuation to higher ground. Miami Beach may opt for vertical evacuation—moving people to the taller hotels. The 65,000 people strung out on the squat, 128-mile-long Florida Keys lack this option; for them, it's get to the mainland on a two-lane causeway or get wet, perhaps fatally so.

Amid such predicaments, a question emerges: Can we learn to control careless urbanization rather than rely on the fortification and nourishment approaches?

Civilization did not have to wait for oceanographic institutes to reveal the beach's fluid, shifting character. Many coastal societies, from the Mediterranean basin to Polynesia, would build homes and settlements well back of the active beach zone to compensate for seasonal shifts and storm surges. They could not rely on federal disaster relief. Taking a cue from this simple method of precaution, Congress, with prodding from environmental and planning groups, has banned most forms of federal aid to *undeveloped* coastal barrier islands, which compose about one-third of our shoreline from Maine to Mexico. In 1990, Congress doubled the area covered by the Coastal Barrier Resources System by adding some 800,000 acres of barrier beaches and associated wetlands. Congress is also extending this system to the Pacific coast.

Given the commercial popularity of the shore, coastal developers still find it profitable to encroach on the beach zone even without federal grants. In some coastal states, including North

Carolina, Oregon, and Florida, new construction must be set back from the active beach zone, and dunes must be preserved. The setbacks anticipate erosion so a home will still be safe decades later. North Carolina and South Carolina have also decided to ban new seawalls, groins, and other "hard" erosion-control devices that subvert the natural sand-transport system and endanger downcoast neighbors. Existing, damaged seawalls are to be phased out. More natural storm-protection devices are being developed. In Bogue Banks, North Carolina, a salt marsh was restored as a wave buffer to protect a shoreline eroding 20 feet per year. Other natural buffers—sand dunes and maritime forests—can also be restored.

The federal government can still remain liable for past errors of coastal development. To reduce the costs of such disaster bailouts, Congress in 1991 was considering measures advocated by Congressmen Thomas Carper (D.–Del.) and Ben Erdreich (D.–Ala.). Repetitive-loss properties, for instance, would be encouraged to rebuild in a manner that would greatly reduce exposure to the next storm, such as a higher building elevation. A National Flood Mitigation Fund would assist communities in relocating disaster-prone properties, restoring protective dunes, and establishing coastal construction setbacks. Some state and local officials complain that such legislation is undue federal involvement in local land use decisions. This criticism overlooks the direct federal interest in reducing a soaring disaster liability. "Why should Uncle Sam's pocketbook be at the mercy of the dune busters, the beach developers, and the mega-resorts?" asks one congressional staff member.

Such coastal initiatives can conserve both beaches and the public purse. Given the tremendous economic gain to be made by subdividing the beach zone, these measures require considerable public support to be implemented. So will measures to maintain sand transport in critical coastal watersheds. The sand and gravel industry competes for diminishing sand sources to meet building construction demands. The industry already extracts sand conveniently impounded behind dams. Sand once carried to the coast by dammed-up stream flows may accumulate in flood-control channels. Coastal regions sometimes dredge out this sand and sell it for a profit, even though their own coastline may be sand-short. (California is trying to implement a "sand rights" concept that would require river sand to be placed on the beach, where it belongs in the first place.) To Dr. Douglas Inman, a beach expert at Scripps Institution of Oceanography, the specter of a sand shortage is the most serious problem in shore management.

The costly legacy of barrier island development will be an instructive reminder of what happens when we take the sandy shore for granted. Italy is having enough trouble with just one Venice; we have built a whole series of Venices along our shore. What goes on in front of and, for that matter, behind the modest beach vegetation line will tell just how well we are learning to respect critical beach processes.

The pressure to build beach resorts in developing nations and tropical islands can trigger a new round of beach erosion. For a small island, loss of the shore may be a prelude to the loss of the land itself. Restoring a beach backed by a bluff or a continent is one thing; restoring a beach backed by a coral atoll or a small coastal plain is another.

Sand transport can become a transnational issue. Some 1,000 square miles of coastal watershed tributary to the California coast lie in Mexico's Baja California. Historically, a border area has supplied sand to San Diego's Imperial Beach. A Mexican dam now disrupts the sand flow, and Imperial Beach has been receding. In the Mediterranean, the sand transport system transcends the borders of Egypt, Israel, and Lebanon. A groin race to rival that of the New Jersey shore could occur here unless the three nations can manage the sand-ocean interface on a multilateral basis.

In 1988, while visiting the small nation of Togo in West Africa, I observed one of the world's worst cases of beach erosion. Over the past decade, the shoreline of West Africa has receded inland by as much as 300 feet. Togo's coastal highway has been relocated inland not once but thrice, a heavy cost for a nation already burdened with development debt. One major erosion cause: a sand-trapping harbor in Lome, Togo, built with development loans from Europe. Another cause: a dam on the Volta River in Ghana that impounds sediments once nourishing the coast of West Africa.

Global warming induced by the greenhouse effect further emphasizes the need for wiser land use and building controls on coastal development. Warm air normally rises into the earth's atmosphere. But scientists are concerned that gasses from fossil fuel combustion can serve to warm air close to the earth's surface. This greenhouse effect could trigger a global warming that would accelerate the melting of polar ice caps and raise global sea levels. There is growing scientific concern that global warming could accelerate the current rise in sea level by as much as three feet over the next century. This sort of rise would hasten the obsolescence of seawalls, docks, groins, and coastal resorts throughout the world. The San Francisco Bay Conservation and Development Commission requires bayside developers to incorporate building elevations and setbacks that account for an accelerated rise in sea level. At the same time, as will be discussed in a later chapter, coastal managers are recognizing the need to support alternative energy policies that could curtail the greenhouse effect.

The challenge of shoreline management arises when I visit a popular summer beach where children can still build sand castles. It is a delight to watch the beach come alive with activity. We are more skilled than ever in the beach arts, from catching a flying disc between our legs to spiking a volleyball or riding a wave. But we still must learn the ultimate skill, living in harmony with such a lively landform. I think we now realize, as never before, the need for this skill, but not the amount of careful effort and planning it entails.

CHAPTER TEN

Living with Killer Waves

I came to the "big island" of Hawaii to see Hawaii Volcanoes National Park. But the bayfront of Hilo proved just as impressive. No high-rise monoliths, commercial strips, or highways separate Hilo from its shore. The shore is predominantly open and green, bisected by a free-flowing river and a fish pond. Picnickers and children with fishing poles outnumber cars and condos. Set back discreetly from this friendly, uncongested waterfront are a commercial district and the homes of the 52,000 Hilo residents who can see, as well as use, their shorefront.

The Hilo shore was once just as cluttered and congested as too many of its urban counterparts. The change agent? A seismic sea wave. The wave—or, to be scientifically accurate, train of waves—occurred one evening in 1960 and killed sixty-one people. More than $22 million worth of property was damaged. Nearly 300 structures were demolished. Noted planner Robert Belt, "Four hundred automobiles, tossed and crushed like tin cans, littered the area; some were bent around trees until the front and rear bumpers met." The scope of damage reflected the fact that downtown Hilo was the shorefront. Like coastal communities on the hurricane-prone Gulf and Atlantic coasts, Hilo was on a collision course with a natural and predictable hazard.

Coastal or submarine earthquakes can displace sea bottom or shore. This displacement energizes waves that can wash ashore thousands of miles away. Globally, these seismic sea waves (tsunamis) are rare compared with other natural hazards. Hawaii, however, rises in the middle of the Pacific Basin, which is rimmed by an active seismic belt. Since 1819, forty-five seismic waves emanating from Alaska, Chile, and Japan have battered Hawaii. Imperceptible in the open ocean, these waves can turn into walls of water fifty or even a hundred feet high at the shore. They occur as a train of waves that may last for thirty minutes or longer. The destructive energy is twofold, resulting from the waves themselves and from wave-driven debris. The shorefront of Hilo literally turned on its residents. Buildings became battering rams.

Time and again, communities punished by floods, earthquakes, hurricanes, and seismic sea waves rebuild in the floodplains, fault zones, and beach areas for a return engagement with disaster. The opportunity to return to familiar surroundings, to be reunited with one's neighbors, and to begin the busy task of rebuilding can reinvigorate citizens shocked by disaster, particularly when federal aid is available. Relocation to new building sites, however safe, can compound the shock. What possessed Hilo to get out of disaster's way?

Hilo ranks as Hawaii's most tsunami-prone community. Reefs help blunt tsunamis along Oahu and other island shores. The island of Hawaii, however, is geologically young. Natural protective barriers have yet to evolve on any large scale. Most island communities, because of the direction their shorelines face, are exposed to tsunamis from only one portion of the seismic belt, whether it be Japan, South America, North America, or New Zealand. Hilo's crescent-shaped bay can accommodate tsunamis from both Alaska and South America. The 1960 wave came from Chile and went on to drown 190 people in Japan. Much of the demolished shorefront was only fifteen years old, rebuilt after a tsunami from Alaska had claimed ninety-six lives in 1946.

The Army Corps of Engineers wanted to tsunami-proof Hilo behind seawalls; however, design specifications—seawalls fifty feet high—were neither affordable nor reliable. Residents were not enchanted with a "superseawall" that would obliterate bay views and make Hilo a "city in a hole." There was also the risk that the superseawall might serve to load the next tsunami with crushing debris. The 1960 wave moved *twenty-ton* boulders from a bayfront revetment hundreds of feet inland.

After the 1946 wave, relocation to higher ground had been suggested. The city settled for a skinny buffer zone and the rock revetment that later turned against the residents. In 1960, the Hawaiian firm of Belt, Collins, and Associates was preparing a city plan for Hilo funded by the U.S. Department of Housing and Urban Development (HUD). When the seismic sea wave hit, this effort was expanded to qualify the damaged area for a redevelopment program. The traditional last resort to disaster mitigation—safer land use—could now become an integral part of public policy.

During the critical planning interim, residents and business-people began to reoccupy the unsafe area and resume their daily activities. Once reestablished, people tend to resist relocation when redevelopment plans materialize. Noted Belt, "Local government restrained individuals from rehabilitating structures and resuming operations which sustained more than 60 percent damage. Putting new construction in place was forbidden for a period of seven months to provide the local government time to formulate rehabilitation plans and a new building code." This foresight meant ultimate relocation of 228 family units and 83 businesses.

Within a year, a plan called Kaiko'o ("Rough Seas") was completed and approved. However tragic the seismic sea wave had been, Hilo now had a singular opportunity to redesign completely both its downtown and its shorefront. The planners reversed the traditional pattern of urban shore use. Of the 350 acres in the project area, 10 were allocated to limited industrial and commercial use, including a commercial fish market and dock. Set at the landward edge of the project area was a 40-acre commercial site raised twenty-six feet above sea level to minimize tsunami exposure.

The remaining 300 acres were kept as a landscaped safety zone. The shift from a sprawling commercial area to a more compact one surrounded by open vistas promised economic dividends. Public services, from streets to drainage systems, could be consolidated. Development controls—including landscaping, underground utilities, and sign standards—could be integrated.

While this plan generated public support, its economic viability was questioned. Local businesspeople lacked the financial resources to develop a completely new commercial site. Outside investment would be required, perhaps from the mainland. Would large investors be attracted to a disaster renewal project named Rough Seas?

To overcome such economic qualms, the county shifted the site for a new $1.7 million headquarters complex to the Kaiko'o site. Next door, the state built a $2.5 million administrative complex.

Such market generators induced an Oahu developer to handle the private end of redevelopment. So that local merchants would have the same credit potential as major chains, the Small Business Administration provided lease payment guarantees to the landlord. Shiigi Drug and Margolis Fashions became neighbors of J. C. Penney and Kress. The local business community now proudly shows visitors the commercial center "born out of disaster." The project earned honorable mention in a 1971 engineering excellence competition of the American Consulting Engineers Council.

Oftentimes, the private portion of a redevelopment project will succeed while the public open-space portion will turn to weeds, as a result of inadequate provisions for maintenance. Permits for temporary commercial use will follow. Park plans will remain paperbound. Kaiko'o has avoided this fate. Formerly the project area contained Liliuokalani Gardens, a Japanese *edo* garden with ponds and picnic grounds, and this was restored. Coconut Island, a palm-fringed islet, was also restored as a picnic ground. Within the project lies Hawaii's shortest river, the Wailoa, less than a half-mile long. The spring-fed river became a state park in 1954. As the Kaiko'o project evolved, the park was expanded to encompass the entire safety zone. Because seismic sea waves can travel up a river mouth and overflow the banks, such expansion provided added safety benefits. Fishing and pleasure-boat facilities, promenades, bike paths, and flower displays now occupy Hilo's former downtown.

Trees and landscaping materials were considered for their relative resistance to tsunamis. Park planners do not want their landscaping materials turned as weapons against Hilo by a future tsunami. Megumi Kon, deputy managing director of the Hawaii Redevelopment Agency, observed in a letter to this writer, "In lieu of the plantings, the wide expanse of open space between the shoreline and the building areas was established. One theory is that the open space would dissipate the energy of the tsunami in the same manner as a wide sand beach does to a large wave."

A sand beach of dazzling black lava grains once rimmed the bay. Seismic sea waves and a bayfront highway contributed to the demise of this distinctive asset. Funds have been set aside to replenish this beach and relocate the bayfront highway; however, according to the county park director, "there is more silt in the bay than sand." Canoe racers and boating enthusiasts have returned to the bay; sewage is no longer discharged into it.

Hilo's modern use of its shorefront is not only safer and more attractive but just as economically productive. Back in 1960, it would have been easier to peddle lava land subdivisions than convince local residents that tax income from Hilo's downtown could be doubled while turning most of that area into a playground. Today, this is the case. What with overall economic growth and Hilo's new access to direct mainland air service, the former downtown—if spared more seismic sea waves—would have prospered, too. But Hilo would be without one of the nation's most beautiful and safe urban waterfronts.

Congress invested more money in Hilo's renewal than it invests in an ordinary disaster relief project—some $6.68 million. When another tsunami hits Hilo, Congress will be asked only to help returf a park, not rebuild a downtown.

Can Hilo's graceful retreat from coastal hazards be utilized elsewhere? Special factors did make Kaiko'o possible. Many urban areas are short of developable land. To relocate to safer ground might mean relocation to another political jurisdiction and an exodus of tax revenues. What city wants to aid competition for its tax base? In Hilo, state-owned undeveloped land was available for the relocation.

The resources of HUD helped expedite Kaiko'o as a redevelopment project. Today, HUD's overall capability to assist urban areas has been drastically cut back. Use of federal disaster relief funds has generally been restricted to the repair of damaged structures and services. Permanent improvement schemes— such as relocation and safety buffer zones—have been discouraged by such stipulations. With repetitive disaster claims adding to the nation's disaster liability, however, there has been a realization that such a policy can be penny-wise and pound-foolish. The *Exxon Valdez* (renamed the *Exxon Mediterranean*), the tanker responsible for the worst oil spill in the United States, was named originally after an Alaskan community that was relocated after the 1964 Good Friday earthquake. At the time, the General Accounting Office criticized federal relief officials for spending $10.5 million to relocate Valdez. Yet a strict policy of "repairs only" would have left the community on a glacial floodplain subject to earthquakes, subsidence, and seismic sea waves. Later, as Alaska's northernmost ice-free port, a Valdez on safer ground would become the pipeline terminal for the huge Arctic oil field—and home port to the massive 1989 tanker oil spill.

Baytown, Texas, enjoys a new "window" to Galveston Bay—a spacious coastal park with beaches and wetlands. This green and blue reserve is the former site of three hundred homes. The site was sinking below sea level; groundwater pumping was causing the homes to sink. Home owners faced repeated coastal flooding. The federal government faced repeated flood insurance claims. Federal officials decided to relocate home owners to safer ground. Baytown transformed a community liability into a regional asset and prime wildlife habitat.

Based in part on lessons learned at Hilo, Valdez, and Baytown, the Federal Emergency Management Agency is now more intent on making hazard mitigation a part of disaster recovery. Once a major disaster occurs, a state/federal hazard mitigation survey team identifies possible land use and building controls that would reduce hazard risks. These reports can open up some interesting planning horizons in our major coastal urban areas. The 1989 Loma Prieta earthquake triggered $6 billion in damage in the San Francisco area. The survey team found that the hard-hit Marina District was sited on a former bay mudflat. During earthquake shaking, these weak, unconsolidated soils can lose their bearing strength and liquefy; the buildings above can sink, split apart, or topple over. This impact had been noted in the 1906 earthquake, but the Bay Area continued to permit development to occur on such soils.

The 1989 earthquake was of only moderate strength. Damage from liquefaction could have been much worse; however, a prolonged drought had lowered the groundwater table, reducing this risk. Recognizing the severe vulnerability of the entire coastal lowlands to the next earthquake, the survey team noted there "is no statewide program requiring local government to regulate development or require special engineering design in those potentially hazardous areas." The federal government provided $3.45 billion in disaster relief for the 1989 earthquake. If California continues to ignore the hazards of weak soils, the next disaster bill could be double that amount.

Although state and local governments are not required to comply with such survey team recommendations, this particular recommendation has not gone unnoticed by community, environmental, and professional groups that for decades have been warning of the danger of ignoring liquefaction risks. These groups now urge that no more wetland and mudflat areas, including diked farmlands, be turned into seismic-prone real estate. Plans to transform an abandoned air force base into a major jetport–industrial complex are being challenged; the old runway is already sinking into wetland soils. Environmental groups would prefer to keep such hazardous lands in agricultural or recreational use or restore them as wildlife and marine habitats. Carefully engineered fills can reduce such hazards but at a cost that can justify high-density development.

If the goal of disaster management is to conserve lives and public funds, such graceful retreats at the coastal edge must become a viable public option. Two centuries of experience with floods, earthquakes, seismic sea waves, and hurricanes affirm that we cannot build the floodwalls high enough, the breakwaters strong enough, or the seawalls long enough to disaster-proof coastal America.

CHAPTER ELEVEN

Deltas in Distress

Frank Ehret, Jr., maneuvers his skiff over the submerged remains of a swamp cypress forest. "I would watch deer here with my dad," the retired schoolteacher explains with a grimace. Today, Ehret's homeland suffers from the fastest rate of land loss on this planet.

Frank Ehret lives in the delta region of Louisiana, which is turning into seabed at the staggering rate of one hundred acres a day. By year's end, up to fifty square miles, an area the size of the District of Columbia, will be underwater. This is one of the more disturbing statistics in the litany of coastal and marine degradation. What is even more disturbing is that Louisiana, like other world-famous delta regions, has yet to learn how to safeguard the shaky ground its citizens walk on.

On a map, the Louisiana delta region hangs like a mudball from the underbelly of North America. From the air, this mudball unfolds into six million acres of green marsh and silvery sheets of water that drift toward the blue sea. Thanks to this squishy wilderness and the people who have colonized it, Louisiana can produce more fish than New England, more furs than

Alaska, more gas than Texas, and more cargo than the Port of New York.

People who work this hard are not supposed to have fun. But don't tell that to the residents of Dulac, Thibodaux, and New Orleans. They may hum "Let the Good Times Roll" as they shrimp, crab, drill, and ring up the cash register. To keep the good times rolling, the people of this delta have taught us jazz, Creole cooking, Mardi Gras, and a stirring lesson in cultural tenacity. Two centuries ago, French-speaking Acadians in eastern Canada came here rather than submit to a British king. To get around in their new marsh wilderness, the Acadians devised the pirogue, a boat with a draft shallow enough to "float on the dew." Today, their descendants—the Cajuns—crew the tugboats, oil rigs, shrimp boats, and barges that reap the delta's rich harvest.

Along the world's shorelines, deltas can emerge where rivers spill over their banks and deposit layers of silt faster than sea waves or currents can wash away the aborning soils. Like the sandy shore, deltas are dynamic, mobile landforms. They can take away as well as give. Restless river channels can shift their course and their life-giving silt loads, forever seeking shorter routes to the sea. Defy or disrupt such dynamic processes and you can pay a heavy price.

Now the day of reckoning approaches for the Louisiana delta. The region, in its economic surge forward, can cut the very ground from underneath its feet. Flood-control levees line the Mississippi River navigation channel on its final run to the Gulf. This leveed channel, a proud achievement of the Army Corps of Engineers, makes New Orleans a major port. It also contributes to the delta's disappearing act. The levees block off the overbank flows that once supplied the delta with silt, nutrients, and fresh water. The channel, deepened for shipping, now carries these life-giving flows past the delta and into the Gulf of Mexico. "The only water that reaches us is rain," says former state legislator Murray Hebert, "and there isn't much silt in rain!"

Some 18,000 miles of canals slice through the delta. The canals, built to reach delta oil fields, permit *salt water* from the advancing Gulf to extend even further into the shrinking delta. Boat wakes from oil barges and recreational craft chew away the soft canal banks. The canals widen. More salt water intrudes. More cypress forests wither.

The delta can *sink* as well as shrink. As billions of tons of oil and gas deposits are pumped out of the ground, ground pressures drop and the land sinks. The marshland above subsides, thus hastening the Gulf's relentless advance. Put together the silt-blocking levees, the marsh-slicing canals, and the deflated land and you have the basic reasons Louisiana is drowning.

Such land loss can sneak up on its potential victims. Lloyd Songe manages the Pointe au Chien Wildlife Management Area. Almost two decades ago, Songe noticed that a favorite deer-hunting area appeared to be going underwater. "I would mention this to my friends," Songe recalls, and they would say, 'Yes, and remember that little canal where we used to fish? You could talk to the person on the other side.' Now it's over 300 feet wide. You'd need a bullhorn to talk." Fishermen began catching marine fish where they once caught freshwater catfish and the state's beloved crayfish. Salt water also began to contaminate municipal water systems.

To scientists, these disturbing signs indicated that the delta was receding before the Gulf at a rate far in excess of natural erosion. In 1970, Dr. Sherwood Gagliano, then with the Center for Wetland Resources at Louisiana State University (LSU), estimated land loss at sixteen square miles per year. Today, Dr. Gagliano—now head of Coastal Environments, Inc., a consulting firm—finds that this rate has nearly *tripled*. The deltaic plain can lose up to fifty square miles yearly; a beach plain that forms southwestern Louisiana loses seven more square miles.

Historically, the lower delta helps buffer the more populated upper delta from the full fury of hurricanes. But as the delta recedes before the advancing Gulf, so does the natural defense line. Buddy Champagne of Theriot hears the sound of coastal

Louisiana drowning when he is in his bed at night. "There is a loud plop and that means another hunk of my property has slumped into the water," he says.

At the current awesome rate of erosion, Dr. Gagliano projects that Plaquemines Parish, home to nearly 30,000 people, could be totally underwater in fifty years, *without any hurricane*. As Billy Tauzin, congressman for the area, explained to his colleagues in Congress, "My district could disappear within the lifetime of my family."

"The Gulf is following us," says Windell Curole, a South Lafourche official proud of his Cajun heritage. "Eventually it could force marsh people to become highlanders."

New Orleans has tended to remain aloof from such harsh delta dilemmas. The city huddles behind a massive, encircling system of "ring" levees built to protect the city from its aquatic neighbors—the Mississippi, Lake Pontchartrain, and the advancing Gulf. But levees alone cannot make up for the loss of Louisiana's natural defense line. In 1965, Hurricane Betsy roared up a newly opened navigation canal (the Mississippi River Gulf Outlet, or "Mr. Go" in local parlance) and swamped eastern New Orleans. Today, with more of its natural buffer gone, the city can expect hurricane storm surges of twenty feet to overtop its existing levee system, according to the National Weather Service.

If this happens—and it could happen now—the city could turn into a deadly bowl of deep water. How deep could the water be if the levees are overtopped by a major hurricane storm surge? "New Orleans would be under fourteen feet of water," observed Dr. Robert Sheets, director of the National Hurricane Center, in testimony to Congress in 1989. The city's spongy delta soils have already subsided as much as twenty feet below sea level. "High ground" in this municipal bowl includes the French Quarter at minus five feet. High-rise buildings peer over the hulking levee system like giant periscopes. Huge turbine pumps must lift rainfall and sewage over the levees so that America's first submarine city will not drown in a downpour or its own effluent. In 1983, one intense downpour overwhelmed the pumps. The city suffered major flood damage and lost telephone contact with the outside world for more than ten hours. Persons needing medical attention, including one pregnant woman due for delivery, resorted to boats to reach hospitals.

"In case of a hurricane storm surge, it could take two months to pump the water out," notes one National Weather Service report. "The potential loss of thousands of lives and billions of dollars worth of property from a severe storm is a very real threat."

The impact of a disappearing delta extends well beyond the boundaries of one state. "If we lose the delta, we would lose one of America's most productive habitats," says David Fruge of the U.S. Fish and Wildlife Service. The delta, which accounts for 25 percent of America's coastal wetlands, sustains more than two-thirds of the Mississippi Flyway's wintering waterfowl (including 400,000 geese) and the country's largest fur and alligator harvest. More than 25 percent of the nation's commercial fish stocks spend part of their life cycle in the fertile delta region.

Today, with a better appreciation of wetlands and muddy waters, Louisiana has created the State Office of Coastal Restoration. In 1988, state voters, by a three-to-one majority, established a wetland restoration fund supported by oil and gas revenues. The Coalition to Restore Coastal Louisiana, composed of one hundred organizations that range from Catholic Social Services to the League of Women Voters, has worked hard to secure such policy initiatives. Sea oats have been replanted on the delta's outer barrier shore to help rebuild dunes. Some abandoned oil canals have been backfilled. In Songe's wildlife area, an abandoned oil canal has been "plugged" with a damlike weir to reduce saltwater intrusion and restrict bank-eroding boat traffic.

In Plaquemines, the parish that could be underwater in fifty years, a control gate has been installed within one levee section. In a project designed to mimic overbank flows of prelevee days, this gate permits river water to be released into the eroding delta rather than wasted to the Gulf. This infusion of "sweet water" is meant to repulse the salty Gulf water that kills freshwater marshland. The Army Corps of Engineers is working on a similar project. The Corps is also evaluating use of dredge spoil to restore wetlands.

Can such projects effectively slow down, much less reverse, the drowning of the delta? It is too early to tell. No coastal region has ever been confronted with such a challenge. There are no textbooks on how to restore a delta reeling from the impacts of a century of runaway development and Faustian engineering. And whatever gains are made can be offset by the state's continued need for revenues from delta development. While some old canals have been plugged, new canals have been built to tap new oil fields. Developers have diked off more delta wetlands and placed more fast tracts in the path of an advancing Gulf. Some experienced observers lean toward pessimism in predicting the delta's future. "We are going to lose south Louisiana," says Dr. Oliver Houck, a law professor at Tulane University. "We are going to be left with a few museums of marsh."

Once again, Uncle Sam can pick up the tab for hazardous coastal development. After Hurricane Juan in 1985, home owners in the delta filed for $50 million in federal flood insurance claims. The levees built to protect their homes were built too low. Warns geologist Dag Nummedal of Louisiana State University, "We should start discouraging development in the lowlands. We cannot afford to lose New Orleans, but we don't want to create other potential traps like it."

Forebodingly enough, one *entire* delta in the United States is already a giant aquatic trap. Much of California's Sacramento–San Joaquin delta has been diked and reclaimed into some sixty island farms. But these synthetic islands sink below sea level as their rich peat soils dry out and blow away. Some island tracts, now at twenty feet below sea level, could drop ten feet more. As the islands sink, their dikes or levees must be raised.

You don't need a Gulf-style hurricane to test the limits of these soggy, sagging levees—high river levels superimposed on high tides can do that. Since 1980, eighteen islands have flooded. Stockton and other cities on the delta rim now find their fates entwined with the sinking delta. If the islands go underwater in domino fashion, the delta could become an inland sea. Waves pound against levees that protect urban tracts. Helicopters and landing craft have been called in to evacuate up to 2,000 residents of flood-threatened islands.

California's sinking delta is a trap for the nation's taxpayers as well. Island owners have received more than $100 million in state and federal disaster aid since 1980 to dewater their farms and repair levees. The cost to close a levee break and dewater a flooded island—$6 million or more—can exceed an island's market value. The Federal Emergency Management Agency (FEMA) has told California that it has "difficulty with justifying" more assistance "unless accelerated progress toward reducing the hazards is achieved." When 1,000-acre Mildred Island flooded in 1983, FEMA rejected requests for disaster aid. Today, people fish where the island once existed. The National Marine Fisheries Service (NMFS) and the Army Corps of Engineers have been working on a plan to convert another sinking island to wetlands to restore rearing habitats for striped bass, steelhead, chinook salmon, and American shad.

The Nile delta contains Egypt's second largest city, Alexandria. The delta also sustains fish and bird stocks shared by the entire Mediterranean region. Its erosion rate jumped dramatically after 1964. The Nile's annual gift of silt now lies 480 miles upriver. The massive Aswan High Dam permits Egyptian farmers to grow three crops a year rather than one. At the same time, the dam, by trapping most of the Nile's silt load, deprives the delta of its muddy "lifeblood." As the delta recedes, the Mediterranean advances. Storm waves undermine a coastal highway and slam into coastal resorts. The advancing Mediterranean now threatens to turn delta lakes into salty arms of the sea.

In the words of one scientist, the silt-trapping dam is delivering a "shock treatment" to the delta. Egypt still feels the Aswan Dam is a net benefit, but its full environmental price lies ahead. According to coastal experts, Egypt must launch a costly crash program to keep its 10,000-square-mile delta region from becoming seabed.

The two rivers that sustain Bangladesh's densely populated delta plain lie largely outside the nation's borders. Neighboring India now diverts river flows from the Ganges to flush silt from Calcutta's port and to irrigate its farms. With river flows too weak to carry the delta's life-giving silt flows, the delta could erode. An anxious Bangladesh seeks to secure agreement on river flows adequate enough to sustain its delta. Lose its delta and Bangladesh loses its nationhood. Already vulnerable to cyclones from the sea, delta residents now find themselves threatened by diversion projects upriver.

In North America, dams on the Colorado River prevent all but a trickle of water from reaching the now historic Colorado delta, located in Mexico below Yuma, Arizona. Once a major port for delta steamboats, Yuma now overlooks a muddy ditch. The upper delta in Mexico is dehydrated; the lower delta is saline, wet only by the tides of the Gulf of California. After extensive and sometimes bitter negotiations, the United States now *pipes* water to Mexico to make up for lost delta flows. (The piped water winds up in Mexican border farms and cities rather than in the dusty delta.)

After World War II, Russia embarked on a dam-building spree to divert flows from the Don, the Volga, and other southern rivers to cropland. With river flows cut by as much as 80 percent, delta regions in the Black, Caspian, and Aral seas have dried up. Fish catches have plummeted. Navigation canals are dry. Municipal sewage collects in barren river channels. Russia must invest in twenty hatcheries to sustain stocks of caviar-bearing sturgeon that have lost their delta spawning grounds. The water level in the Aral Sea has dropped by seven feet. The shore now generates dust rather than fish.

Russia's devastating experience with delta-killing dams is not lost on American scientists. Conveners of a 1980 National Symposium on Fresh Water Inflow to Estuaries concluded that "no more than 25 to 30 percent of the historic river flow can be diverted without disastrous ecological consequences" to the receiving estuary or delta. Dr. Michael Rozengurt, a Russian marine scientist who now lives in San Francisco, warns that water supply withdrawals can disrupt the ecosystem of the California delta, already reeling from the impacts of subsidence. In 1991, the Environmental Protection Agency was threatening to impose water standards to protect the delta if California did not do so. At the same time, state officials were criticizing another federal agency, the Bureau of Reclamation, for diverting delta river flows to rice and cotton farmers at subsidized rates despite the delta's deteriorating condition.

Louisiana could reintroduce river flows to its eroding delta, only to see dam projects in the upper river basin capture more of these flows to meet future water demands. Dr. Gagliano already foresees the need to ensure adequate flows to the lower basin before diversion projects in the upper basin get out of hand.

Like our beaches, our deltas can no longer be taken for granted. As our power to build bigger dams, deeper ship channels, and longer levees increases, so does our power to choke off silt flows and sweet water that sustain these dynamic and now endangered landforms. While scientists and environmental groups have been warning us for more than a decade to recognize the plight of our deltas, in practice we still continue to regard them as being as expendable as a spent mine or a cut forest. Their future existence remains subordinate to upstream water demands, ship navigation, and oil development. Despite the Bush administration's national goal of no net loss of wetlands, America's major wetland region continues to drown.

The survival of a region that Frank Ehret once celebrated with his father may require more direct federal action. After a decade of disaster bailouts, the United States is joining in the effort to see if the natural delta can be restored. In 1990, Congress agreed to provide up to $30 million a year to restore delta wetlands. In return for such assistance, Congress should expect Louisiana to rigorously enforce controls on new canals and other delta-destroying activities. If Louisiana is not prepared to safeguard the land it walks on, why should the general taxpayer be? If the United States, with its level of scientific and technical expertise, can't muster the political will to salvage such a productive delta, the prognosis for other deltas around the world is going to be grim indeed.

PART FOUR

The Toll of Pollution

CHAPTER TWELVE

The Long, Sticky Reach of Oil

The sea winds were blowing onshore, cooling off a million weekend bathers escaping the hot August heat. But this breezy salvation for a sweltering southern California bothered the Coast Guard official. "You don't want these winds when a tanker spills oil," he explained to me. "With winds like this, the skimmers are useless and the spill gets legs, real long legs." The fallback plan for this, I learned, would be to boom off three major ports, call off naval maneuvers, move some sea otters to onshore safety, and mobilize a work crew of 5,000 to hand-clean some 400 miles of the world's most photogenic coastline.

That high-tech, high-flying California could be momentarily brought down on its economic knees by the long reach of spilled oil is but one example of how coastal regions find themselves entangled in the strengths and weaknesses of one industrial enterprise. Oil has fueled the industrial revolution and become a key element in our life-style. Today, though, its benefits can be offset, if not overtaken, by its rising environmental price for those who live and work along the coastal rim.

For the oil industry, the coastal zone is an extended workplace. Here are the ports to receive oil, the refineries to process it, the tank farms to store it, the pipelines to ship it inland and keep our cars and trucks rolling. Here, too, begin the sea-lanes to ship oil around the world. And here begins the new "frontier"—the offshore oil fields to prolong our hydrocarbon existence as onshore reserves run out.

Today, the ports of Los Angeles, San Francisco, and New York each host about 1,000 tanker visits a year. Some 4,000 oil platforms dot the new frontier, from the chilly waters of Alaska to the humid Gulf of Mexico. Three hundred additional artificial islands pump more oil. In the Gulf of Mexico, the busiest marine frontier, some 25,000 kilometers of oil pipelines crisscross the seabed and coastal wetlands.

And that's only a dress rehearsal for the future. The oil industry wants to open up such new frontier areas as Georges Banks off Massachusetts, the waters off Washington and Oregon, and, in Alaska, the Beaufort and Bering seas and the Arctic National Wildlife Refuge. From Norway to China, other nations rush to open up their frontiers, often in joint ventures with U.S. oil firms, the pioneers and leaders in offshore oil technology. "We need it all," explained a Unocal executive eager to explore some thirty-nine new offshore tracts along California's Central Coast. "That's what we need to sustain our way of life."

For most of this century, coastal regions have been willing to accommodate such marine visions. For Louisiana, Texas, and Alaska, offshore oil royalties can reduce or eliminate the need for state income taxes or property taxes. For Uncle Sam, oil revenues from the outer continental shelf (the area beyond state jurisdiction) are second only to income taxes as a revenue source.

There were some early omens that the rush into the marine frontier could backfire. In 1967, despite a clear day, calm waters, high tide, excellent charts, a warning flare from a lighthouse ship, and a sterling 100A1 rating from Lloyd's insurers, the *Torrey Canyon* still slammed into Seven Stones Reef to become a historic shipwreck. The cargo of the tanker was a liquid one, totaling thirty-six million gallons, ordinarily a raindrop in the vast solution of the ocean. But the ocean cannot absorb oil very efficiently. Within three days, slicks the color of melted chocolate sprawled over a hundred square miles of ocean, a moving quagmire that ensnared seabirds by the thousands. The slicks, with their cargo of flightless birds, rolled up on the golden beaches of Cornwall and the pink granite coast of Brittany. As no coastal storm could ever do, this oil-smeared sea incapacitated the coasts of two nations and defied cleanup efforts.

In 1969, another style of oil spill made its debut, the offshore oil blowout that can coat 800 square miles of nearshore and smear thirty miles of beach, as happened in the Unocal blowout off Santa Barbara, California. Despite such troublesome omens, coastal regions continued to accept more development on the burgeoning marine frontier. The oil industry that had the expertise to build supertankers longer than football fields and oil platforms taller than the Empire State Building said it would develop the technology to clean up the next spill. Regulatory agencies told the oil industry to prepare spill contingency plans. Some critics urged that the thin-skinned tankers be equipped with double hulls to reduce the risk of spills from the next collision. Such urgings were largely ignored.

But the specter of spills and of inadequate or tardy control efforts persisted. The 1978 *Amoco Cadiz* spill off France and the 1979 Ixtoc-1 blowout in Mexico that reached as far north as Texas reaffirmed the limits of relying on impromptu cleanups. Were damaging spills really an unavoidable price that coastal regions would have to learn to accept?

In 1989, the spill that wasn't supposed to happen did happen. The *Exxon Valdez*, now named *Exxon Mediterranean*, ran into Bligh Reef in Alaska's Prince William Sound and spilled eleven million gallons of Arctic crude. This spill could not be blamed on the prototype "rust bucket" tanker able to skimp on safety by being flagged in Liberia. This was a vessel owned and operated by the largest oil company in the United States and subject to regulation by Alaska and the United States. Some 1,200 miles of shore would receive an oily absolution. About 33,000 seabirds would be killed. So would 1,000 sea otters. The cleanup technology for such a large spill simply wasn't there.

Or, for that matter, anywhere. In March 1990, the *American Tanker* punctured its hull with its anchor while preparing to unload more Alaskan crude. This time the spill recipient would be the coastline of Orange County, California. The skimmers materialized faster than at Valdez, and the winds were initially cooperative. The amount of oil spilled—400,000 gallons—was much less than that from the *Valdez*. Yet only 20 percent would be recovered at sea. Too much wound up on birds—some 700 died—and along a fifteen-mile stretch of sandy beach, one of the busiest and most popular of all sandy shores in the world. This stretch of beach had to close down for a month as the shores were hand-cleaned, oil glob by oil emulsion. As Coast Guard Commandant Admiral Paul Yost told local reporters, "I'm not satisfied with the skimming capability we have in the United States—especially the high seas capability. We don't have enough." If an industrial nation like the United States is so defenseless, you can imagine where this leaves coastal regions like the Caribbean, exposed to extensive tanker traffic.

The 20 percent recovery rate, while not adequate to protect either wildlife or the beaches, was a smash performance compared with most efforts at spill control. According to a 1990 Office of Technology Assessment study, booms and skimmers can recover only about 10 percent of oil spilled. Moreover, this technology works only under limited conditions. Based on actual tests, the California Coastal Commission found that skimmers and other cleanup equipment are not effective in waves higher than six feet or in currents of more than one knot—conditions that can prevail off southern California 25 percent of the time and in central and northern California 50 to 80 percent of the time. Use of chemical dispersants to "sink" spills can create toxic problems. Burning of spills can be limited by weather and the need to initiate burning before the slick spreads too thinly. Thus, two decades after the *Torrey Canyon* and Santa Barbara spills and despite the repeated assurances of the oil industry and its regulators, coastal regions still find themselves hostage to the shortcomings of marine oil development.

Presumably, the threat of liability for damages might stimulate better prevention and control strategies; however, this threat, like the "sea dragons" of cleanup technology, can turn out to be a paper tiger. The oil industry and most industrial nations have been willing to abide by international conventions that establish uniform liability standards for tankers . . . if the liability is limited. While the potential for damage from a major spill can exceed $2 billion, the conventions developed by the International Maritime Organization limit liability to $60 million for large tankers. And this liability focuses on cleanup costs, not damage to natural and public resources.

Rather than ratify such a porous safeguard, the U.S. Congress has tried, since 1980, to establish a higher ceiling for tanker traffic in U.S. coastal waters. The American Petroleum Institute, an oil industry lobbying group, would go along with this measure . . . if Congress would preempt the standard of unlimited liability invoked by some nineteen coastal states. Given the shortcomings of cleanup technology and the value of the resources at risk (in California, coastal tourism generates $16 billion in revenues annually; commercial fishing, an additional $2 billion), coastal states understandably want such legal protection. While the oil industry claims such a provision weakens or eliminates its ability to obtain marine insurance, tankers continue to visit California and other states that retain unlimited liability.

It took the 1989 *Exxon Valdez* spill and a series of 1990 spills in New York Harbor, Galveston Bay, and Orange County to finally get Congress to raise liability limits and to create a $1 billion cleanup fund without preempting stiffer state standards.

Congress also finally decided to override industry objections and require double hulls. The oil industry has until the year 2010 to comply with this tardy concession to tanker safety.

But the oil industry did gain one victory. The shipowner, not the owner of the spilled oil, is the party responsible for damages. In 1990, Shell declared it would cease shipping oil to the United States in its tanker fleet except for an offshore terminal in the Gulf of Mexico. Shell's reason: to avoid the risk of rising liability for spill damages. By reducing its risk, Shell raises the risks for coastal states. Most shipowners lack the financial resources of oil firms. Some are corporations whose only asset is one tanker. "Who wants to fight an oil spill backed up by the value of a holed tanker resting on the seabed," notes one coastal manager. Fortunately for Alaska, Exxon, the owner of the *Valdez,* happened to own the oil, too. Otherwise, Alaska and the federal government might have been stuck with a grounded tanker and a $2 billion cleanup bill.

The federal bill, along with industry plans to set up regional spill centers, will help advance spill control. Such incremental advances, however, can be offset by the changing nature of the offshore frontier. There is now more to run into or damage, whether it be aquaculture pens, naval maneuvers, recreational armadas, whale-watching boats, offshore oil platforms, or more oil tankers. To coastal states, the marine frontier is shaping up as a rather stressed environment that needs more protection and less runaway development.

To reduce the demand for imported oil and the risks of more tanker spills, the oil industry has an answer: Accelerate the oil leasing of offshore America. To coastal states, however, this idea seems to be a case of going out of the frying pan and into the fire. Spills from oil platforms can be just as hard to control as those from tankers. And the promise of replacing tankers with platforms can, like spill control, be illusory. In deeper-water areas, platform producers may find it cheaper to tanker their crude rather than pipe it onshore. As a result, some offshore leases could *increase* tanker traffic and the risk of spills. In a 1989 federal impact report, coastal officials in central California learned that one proposed lease sale would increase tanker traffic by 41 percent, or 400 more tanker transits per year at peak production. At least four major accidents could be expected, including a tanker spill, a platform spill, and at least two serious pipeline leaks. This seems like a curious way to save our seas from slips by foreign tankers.

Offshore oil fields can stain more than water. According to the California State Air Resources Board, nitrogen emissions from one exploratory drilling vessel are equivalent to those from 11,000 autos. Airborne pollution from large oil fields could put some coastal counties in violation of federal air standards and subject to federal grant cutoffs. Federal offshore oil fields were not even subject to federal air standards until Congress changed this situation in the 1990 Clean Air Bill.

The oil industry does not always appreciate a heightened sensitivity to the risks it can impose on coastal neighbors. Santa Barbara County, site of the 1969 blowout and now next door to some twenty offshore oil platforms, wanted Chevron Company to pipe rather than tanker its crude from a new project to refineries in Los Angeles. Chevron agreed to this step as part of a county permit, built a $2 billion platform and onshore separation unit, and then decided it wanted to revert to the tankers. But the county balked. After all, the oil industry itself proclaims that pipes are safer than tankers. For adhering to this safety-first policy, the county saw itself castigated on national television, when the 1990 Middle East crisis broke, for contributing to our dependence on imported oil and, by implication, the need for our sons and daughters to defend Saudi oil fields. The critic: a spokesperson for Chevron, who claimed the county was responsible for holding up production on its new platform.

In this manner, the risks of oil development can be justified on the basis of national security. California Congressman William Dannemeyer would rather accelerate offshore leasing than explain to parents why "their sons are fighting on the sands of Middle East oil fields to retain oil supplies." Thus, coastal states find their future enmeshed in the geopolitics of the Middle East as well as in the plans of oil firms and federal budget officials. With offshore oil development enshrined as a national security imperative, oil can continue to seek preemptions from strong standards on tanker safety, air and water pollution, wetland protection, and liability. Indeed, the repeated push for such preemptions suggests that the oil industry cannot adjust to the needs of a protected and restored coastal zone . . . or the emergence of solar, wind, conservation and other low-risk, low-polluting competitors.

To many coastal states, this is reason enough to shift to energy strategies that don't require coastal zones to become sacrificial oil patches. Once again, however, the federal response to this policy option can be tardy if not downright antagonistic. During the Reagan administration, federal initiatives in energy conservation and renewable sources were cut back or eliminated. As a result, the United States lost its technical lead in areas like photovoltaic solar cells to Japan and West Germany. The Bush administration has increased its support for renewable energy but not at levels that will enable the United States to regain its lost leadership. In early 1991, the Bush administration submitted to Congress a much-delayed national energy plan that tilts toward more oil production and more oil consumption. More nuclear power is envisioned, too, even though the United States has yet to figure out how to safely dispose of an existing backlog of radioactive garbage. A *Los Angeles Times* editorial described this policy tilt as "a policy blackout and intellectual failure."

Rather than be pawns in energy politics, coastal states have learned how to encourage energy strategies more compatible with a safe coastal zone. California, Massachusetts, and Florida have carried on and expanded alternative energy programs the federal level has neglected. In 1990, the California Public Utilities Commission required the state's four major utilities to undertake an extensive rebate program that will pay users to use less energy by buying more efficient appliances. In the first year, this conservation thrust will save 250 megawatts of electricity at half the cost of building a power plant with this capacity. California State Senator Gary Hart (D.–Santa Barbara) wants to extend this concept to automobile fuel efficiency. His proposed "drive plus" bill would provide rebates to drivers who buy high-mileage cars; the rebates would be funded by taxes on drivers who buy gas-guzzling models. At the same time, the California Energy Commission has continued to fund programs to help develop wind, solar, and geothermal energy resources.

Coastal states can also raise the ante for repeated spills, large or small. In 1988, a tank owned by Shell Oil leaked, spilling oil into coastal wetlands and San Francisco Bay. Dikes to contain such spills were built too low. While not a big spill, the event still involved enough oil to damage wetland habitat, injure birds, and interrupt fishing, birding, and boating. By ascertaining the value of lost wildlife and lost opportunities in coastal activities and adding this amount to cleanup costs, California Attorney General John Van De Kamp, working with federal resource agencies, secured a $20 million settlement from Shell, much higher than the normal assessment for spills larger in size and impact. This settlement will enable California to restore degraded wetland habitat to compensate for the spill impact and for interruption of coastal activities. In 1990, Congress directed the National Oceanographic and Atmospheric Administration to upgrade the federal government's ability to recover such damages and implement restoration plans.

Through their congressional delegations, coastal states can temper the federal ardor for offshore oil leases. After vigorous lobbying by coastal legislators including California's Senator-turned-Governor Peter Wilson, President Bush agreed to a ten-year delay in new leases off much of California and all of southwestern Florida, Washington, Oregon, and New England. Because of a future change of administration or heart, coastal states would like this pledge to be enacted as law.

At the same time, coastal states have been stepping up their lobbying for federal conservation initiatives. An increase in federal auto fuel efficiency standards of just two more miles of gas per gallon could save more oil than the Arctic National Wildlife Refuge could produce.

If the long-standing hazards of marine oil development don't drive home the need for such energy alternatives, a newer hazard may. Global warming, by inducing rising sea levels, may eventually threaten Miami and other low-lying coastal regions. A major cause of global warming, carbon dioxide (CO_2) emissions, is the burning of fossil fuels. Coastal states that are being urged to expedite offshore oil leasing are in effect being asked to play host to the very energy source that could drown their beaches, mangrove forests, coral reefs, and cities, inch by rising inch of sea level.

Once again, the federal response to this all-encompassing hazard seems somewhat anemic. Sea-girded Europe is ready to sign an international treaty to cut carbon dioxide levels by 20 percent by the year 2010. The United States, the world's biggest CO_2 emitter, is not. To the Bush administration, scientific uncertainty over global climate change is too great to justify the cost of remedial measures. While models to predict global climate change have their shortcomings, European nations regard the evidence as sobering enough to act now. Paying a carbon tax or shifting to more fuel-efficient cars seems like a small price to keep London, Venice, and Holland dry. The more action is delayed, the less chance to slow down, much less reverse, the rise in CO_2 emissions.

In the United States, coastal states will need to play an increasing role in shaping a prudent federal response to such a critical issue. Coastal legislators like Senate Majority Leader George Mitchell (D.–Maine) support the need for a more farsighted response. In 1992, a United Nations Conference on Conservation and Development in Brazil will consider global action to cut CO_2 emissions. The United States and other industrial nations may eventually be able to gain credits for required CO_2 emission cuts by transferring renewable and energy-efficient technologies to developing nations. By helping to cultivate such energy options, coastal states like California and Hawaii have demonstrated that energy policy need not be on a collision course with a safe environment.

CHAPTER THIRTEEN

Seas of Slime, Seas of Death

You must place them under a microscope to see them. Then these tiny marine organisms, encased in intricate silicon skeletons, glitter like miniature jewel boxes. Select members of the plankton family, these delicate-appearing organisms can discolor the sea, kill marine animals by the thousands, and turn summer resort seasons into a stinking shambles.

Red tide is the popular name for such havoc. Red tides were once considered freakish events triggered by rouge plankton species content to keep a low profile most of the time. Over the past two decades, however, this attitude has been jolted. Scientists have observed that toxic or noxious red tides are occurring more often and are spreading to coastal regions that previously never experienced their impacts. While better reporting is given some credit for this trend, there is growing evidence that our own actions can tilt the balance toward a global epidemic of such noxious tides.

The phenomenon of "discolored water"—the scientifically accepted phrase for red tide—has been occurring in a variety of shades throughout much of the planet's history. The *Iliad* spoke of the Mediterranean's changing color, and the seventh chapter of Exodus observed the same chameleonlike quality on the lower Nile:

> And all of the waters that were in the river were turned to blood and the fish that was in the river died; and the river stank, and the Egyptians could not drink of the water of the river.

The sea can and does turn white off Ceylon, yellow off Brazil, green off Spain, and dull red off California and Alaska. The sea turns red off Peru, but Peruvians call the lethal tide el pintor, in honor of the sulfurous fumes of accompanying decay that blacken ship's brass.

Since the late 1940s, the Florida Gulf Coast has been experiencing a red tide outbreak once every two years. The responsible organism, Ptychodiscus brevis, belongs to the dinoflagellates (whirling organisms with whiplike appendages), a very talented member of the plankton family. Like plants, dinoflagellates use sunlight to transform sea nutrients into energy (photosynthesis). Like animals, dinoflagellates are mobile, driven by currents, winds, and their slim appendages.

Under the right conditions, these tiny animals can burst into frantic fertility. Counts of P. brevis in a quart of seawater can jump from 1,000 to 60 million. These blooms are so dense that the water is slimy to the touch. Depending on pigments of the multiplying organisms, the sea turns red, yellow, or even green.

Some red tide blooms are relatively benign. Others are toxic, and P. brevis falls into this fatal category. P. brevis blooms excrete a toxin that immobilizes a fish's nervous system, including its gills. This nerve toxin accounts for the spasmodic motion of mullet and other finfish just before death. The massive decomposition that results from the fish pogroms has another lethal aspect: The process of decomposition itself exhausts the oxygen content of the water and serves to suffocate fish and shellfish that have not yet taken in the toxin.

Like a massive janitor's broom, the tides and the winds sweep fish windrow after fish windrow onto the glistening white Gulf beaches. Municipal bulldozers and road scrappers hastily push the stinking, sun-basted windrows into lime-filled pits. An odorless and colorless gas swirls above this makeshift burial ground; beach visitors and vendors gasp, gag, and even vomit.

The bloom dies off and the waters turn blue again. But the danger is far from over. Clams and other filter-feeding shellfish can consume the bloom organisms and accumulate the biotoxins. Although these biotoxins are not necessarily lethal to the shellfish, people who harvest the shellfish can suffer a nerve disorder called paralytic shellfish poisoning (PSP). As a result, Florida enacts bans on shellfish harvesting during red tide outbreaks.

Along the California coast, shellfish can concentrate a toxin that is 100,000 times as potent as cocaine and is carried by another red tide dinoflagellate (*Protogonyaulax catenella*). So far, thirty-eight persons who have consumed mussels containing this powerful nerve toxin have died. Boiling contaminated shellfish will not destroy this powerful toxin. California bans harvest of shellfish from May to September because of the potential presence of *P. catenella*. (The nerve toxin in *P. brevis* is not considered fatal.) Other red tide dinoflagellates can carry a toxin that causes acute stomach illness in consumers of shellfish. This illness is called diarrhetic shellfish poisoning (DSP).

A series of natural events is associated with many red tide outbreaks. A heavy rainfall may be followed by calm seas and steady sunshine. Runoff may generate nutrients necessary to sustain massive blooms. The runoff may also contain crucial trace compounds, such as vitamin B_{12} and chelated iron. Until the early 1970s, most scientists felt that these events were well beyond our influence and that red tides were as natural as earthquakes and the budding of flowers.

Events in Japan's Seto Sea jolted this certitude. Once considered a rare occurrence here, red tides suddenly became all too common during the 1970s. By 1976, a record 326 tides were reported. Not all were toxic, but those which were racked up considerable damage. With Japan running out of wild stocks to sustain its seafood demands, the Seto Sea is a prime aquaculture center for finfish like bream and yellowtail. In 1987, one toxic tide killed one million yellowtail.

Scientists trying to understand this deadly epidemic of tides noticed in the late 1970s that the chemistry of the seawater was changing. Red tide organisms ordinarily deplete the waters of nutrients like nitrogen and phosphorus and thus starve themselves to death. But levels of these nutrients remained high and were even on the increase. The dramatic increase in the tides coincided with an upsurge in industrial and urban sewage discharges. Could nutrients in the sewage be fueling these deadly blooms? Some scientists said these nutrient loads would have to be reduced or the sea would become a virtual bowl of toxic tides. Other scientists contended that natural causes alone were at work. With its emerging aquaculture industry at risk—fish farmers lost some thirty million yellowtail to toxic tides in Seto Sea from 1970 to 1988—Japan decided it had no choice but to put these two opposing perspectives to the test. The government ordered cities and industry to cut back on their nutrient loads. One prime nutrient source—phosphate in detergents—was banned. With these measures instituted, rate of tides dropped from the peak of 326 in 1976 to some 200 today. The Japanese experience in Seto Sea suggests that our nutrient loads can indeed change the biological composition of bays and semienclosed seas, tipping the balance toward tiny organisms fatal to our marine ambitions.

Tolo Harbor, a long, narrow bay in Hong Kong, recorded its first red tide in 1971. By 1980, tides were becoming a regular event. In the summer of 1987, one noxious tide killed 120 tons of fish, including cultured species. By 1988, the tides were occurring almost year-round. As in the case of Seto Sea, researchers linked the epidemic of tides to an upsurge in urban growth and a corresponding jump in nutrient-rich sewage loads. Hong Kong officials are now trying to reduce the nutrient loads to cut the tide rate. Once willing to write off *P. brevis* blooms as purely natural events, Florida officials are now investigating whether spiraling sewage loads contribute to the development and duration of toxic blooms.

Other coastal regions find themselves enmeshed in the epidemic of tides. In 1972, southern New England experienced its first toxic tide. "Every year since that event, PSP has occurred in that region, often in historically popular clamming areas," notes Dr. Donald Anderson, a red tide expert at Woods Hole Oceanographic Institute in Massachusetts.

In 1987, coastal residents in North Carolina experienced severe eye and respiratory irritation as sea breezes turned noxious. Fish began to float belly-up. North Carolina was experiencing its first toxic tide. The triggering organism was the one associated with toxic tides along the Florida Gulf Coast. Scientists feel that *P. brevis* reached North Carolina by hitchhiking on the northward-flowing Gulf Stream; they now wonder if *P. brevis* may migrate even further north and invade the Chesapeake Bay region, already beset with declining resource stocks.

In 1985, Long Island experienced its first brown tide. The causative organism was a member of the phytoplankton family. While not toxic, the brown tide is still harmful. "Its blooms are so dense that shellfish either stop filtering or retain very little food and starve to death," reports Dr. Anderson. "The blooms also block the sunlight and thus destroy eelgrass beds, an important habitat for scallops and other marine organisms." The brown tide reoccurred in 1986 and 1987. Long Island's scallop industry was virtually wiped out by the brown tides; it has yet to recover. Scientists are unsure to what degree these brown tides are natural or human-induced and whether they will return.

In 1989, Italian beach resorts in the Upper Adriatic began offering vacation rebates to entice tourists. The region has suffered a severe drop in tourism because of waters turned green and slimy by repeated algal tides. Such tides have occurred in the past but have not been of such enduring intensity. The upsurge is attributed to land-based pollution; Italian authorities are attempting to reduce sewage loads, particularly from the Po River watershed, which drains major industrial cities.

The Baltic, another semienclosed sea, copes with noxious algal tides that smother beaches in foul-smelling foams. Excess nutrients from sewage and from fertilizer-rich farm runoff are linked to the increase in these foul tides. "We have a green hand in the sea," Victor Smetacek, a marine biologist in Bremerhaven, Germany, told a reporter for *Science* in 1990.

These algal tides, with their affinity for inshore coastal waters, preempt major recreational, scenic, and fishery resources. Aquaculture is counting on such waters to increase the harvest of cultured seafood, but, thanks to our sewage loads, we seem to be culturing toxic tides as well. Ironically, aquaculture projects may be part of the problem. Salmon pens and other finfish projects can generate nutrient-rich wasteloads of their own, including fish feces and uneaten food pellets. Norway is beginning to limit the number of salmon pens in its fjords to prevent a buildup of such wastes. Hong Kong is limiting the number of finfish pens in its troubled Tolo Harbor. "Whereas pig wastes can be hosed away, you cannot do the same thing in aquaculture zones," notes Hong Kong marine scientist Brian Morton. (At one time, sewage outfall operators were claiming that their sewage loads only helped to fertilize the seas, not anticipating that "bad" species, rather than treasured sport fish, could benefit the most.) Some scientists are also concerned that cultured finfish in sea pens may graze down more benign plankton species, thereby favoring survival of more toxic species.

Unlike waste-producing salmon and shrimp farms, seaweed and oyster farms *remove* nutrients from the water column. Pilot projects are now under way to see if seaweeds and filter-feeding oysters can help cleanse nutrient-rich waste streams from salmon pens and shrimp ponds. Depending on the results, single-species mariculture may give way to mutually beneficial salmon-oyster-seaweed polyculture.

Other scientists identify more ways by which we may be

overfeeding the marine ecosystem. In 1988, the Environmental Defense Fund in New York City fingered an airborne "enrichment" source: nitrogen and phosphorus emitted from power plant smokestacks that ultimately settle on the sea surface.

As noxious tides and enrichment sources proliferate, nations that once ignored research into tiny organisms with confusing Latin names now begin to realize their significance. In 1974, the first international conference on toxic blooms attracted participants from three countries; by 1987, this conference was attracting participants from twenty-seven countries.

Clearly, we have much to learn about how noxious algal blooms form and spread. "The reason that some noxious or toxic phytoplankton dominate other species in polluted waters remains a mystery," Dr. Anderson has observed. "But the fact remains that man's activities in the coastal zone can directly affect the incidence of red tides." Calm summer seas and steady sunshine, once the delight of beach visitors, can now become a disturbing omen in Seto Sea, the Baltic, and the Upper Adriatic. To what extent these regions will have to reduce their sewage loads or live with slimy seas remains uncertain. While initial reductions have lowered the rate of tides in the Seto Sea, the region still has to cope with 200 tides a year. Other regions, like North Carolina and Long Island, wonder whether their "freakish" tides will turn into routine events.

Regions rarely if ever touched by noxious tides, even areas far inland, can nevertheless be affected. As the global appetite for seafood expands, the need to monitor and prevent seafood contaminated with PSP or DSP from entering markets becomes even more critical. To ensure a safer ocean, we must now learn what are the parameters of a proper marine diet for organisms we cannot even see with our naked eye. Before this experience is over, farmers, city dwellers, and power plant operators hundreds of miles away from sea breezes may find their way of doing things changed. This is not the only aquatic boomerang from our use of the ocean as an all-purpose dump.

CHAPTER FOURTEEN

Swamped by Sewage

Jogging along the Boston shore one morning, William Golden noticed what appeared to be jellyfish exposed by the low tide. The next moment he was disgusted—then angered. "The jellyfish turned out to be shiny clumps of human fecal matter and grease," recalls the jogging lawyer. Like thousands of other shore lovers, Golden was getting a firsthand look at America's sewage system in action.

It is a system that has transformed too many of our bays and coastal waters into public health time bombs and environmental cripples. From coast to coast, millions of gallons of raw, murky sewage can leak through pipes, gush out of manholes, back up in basements, and wash up onto our shores, along with hospital needles and tons of plastic debris that can endure for 400 years.

These runaway wasteloads can make our beaches unsafe and turn our shellfish into public health hazards. Repeated beach closings in 1988 cost the states of New Jersey and New York some $2 billion in lost vacation and business revenues. In the past decade, progress has been made in controlling some of the worst holes in our sewage system. But much remains to be done if we no longer want to rely on beach and shellfish-bed closures as a standard management tool.

The struggle against our spiraling wasteloads has never been an easy one. The huge sewage disposal plants that sprawl along our urban waterfronts are, in a way, concrete memorials to a sewage strategy developed a century ago. In the nineteenth century, as our cities expanded in the industrial age, human sewage displayed its awesome power to thwart material progress. Soaring wasteloads overwhelmed "on-site" disposal systems— outhouses, septic tanks, and gutters that drained into the nearest river or bay. New York, Boston, and San Francisco reeled from typhoid, cholera, and other sewage-spawned epidemics. On-site systems gave way to a system of piping sewage to off-site or central plants. While designed to remove some gross sewage matter, these plants still relied on our waterways to dilute and "purify" the mounting urban waste streams. The urban shift to waterborne disposal—from six-gallon toilet flush to million-gallon-a-day outfall discharge—was in full force.

With local water bodies used as sewage sinks, booming coastal cities extended their water pipes to out-of-state watersheds. Boston reached out to the Connecticut River, New York City to the Delaware. Semiarid Los Angeles would develop the most extended water reach—into Owens Valley in excess of 400 miles. First intended to supplement local sources, imported water became the predominant source as urban growth boomed. Local surface and subsurface water supplies came to be polluted.

By the 1960s, reliance on waterborne disposal showed signs of breaking down. Rising wasteloads exceeded the cleansing ability of our waterways. From Coney Island to San Francisco, quarantine signs reappeared on our waterfronts. Toxic wastes augmented the polluting prowess of human sewage. While wasteloads increased, purifying flows in our rivers were being reduced. In California, dams and pumps began to divert up to 40 percent of the historic river flows into the San Francisco Bay delta system. In Texas, the Trinity and other rivers could carry more treated effluent than natural water. Polluted runoff from urban streets, cattle feedlots, and farmland ("nonpoint sources") competed with sewage outfalls for whatever cleansing ability our waterways can still muster.

In 1972, a worried Congress responded with the federal Clean Water Act. The Environmental Protection Agency (EPA) was given a big stick—the power to set and enforce discharge standards into the nation's waterways—and a very big carrot—the power to dispense federal grants for sewage treatment. One purpose of the grant program was to encourage wastewater reuse and other alternatives to conventional waterborne disposal. As a leading sponsor of the act, Senator Edmund Muskie (D.–Maine) noted at the time that our waterways should no longer be considered part of the waste treatment process.

Unfortunately, our waterways still remain so—despite an infusion of $52 *billion* in federal sewer grants. While federal funding has escalated, our strategy against pollution has tended to stagnate. For the most part, federal funds have made our sewer plants bigger and the outfalls longer, thus *increasing* our reliance on conventional waterborne disposal. According to the EPA, water quality has actually declined in many bays and coastal waters. Population growth strains the capacity of coastal waters to handle pollutants. Today, one-half of our population lives on or near the coasts.

Today, each of us generates about sixty gallons of wastewater daily. And the greater the wasteloads pouring into treatment plants, the more cleansing steps are necessary before disposal. Primary treatment—removal of floating debris and some suspended solids—must escalate to secondary treatment—an elaborate process using bacteria to remove more solids. But this latter method generates tons of sludge that settle out from the waste stream. And the waste stream itself can still contain nutrients that trigger noxious "blooms" of pea-soup algae. Result: another chemical and biological treatment to remove algae-feeding nitrogen and phosphorus.

The whole process creates risks of larger and larger acciden-

tal spills from giant plants. The first truly massive spill burst
from a model San Jose–Santa Clara, California, sewer plant in
1979. Fishermen in the southern San Francisco Bay watched
the water turn brown. For a month, billions of gallons of mar-
ginally treated human sewage gushed into the bay. Fishing,
boating, and swimming had to be restricted. As the area fought
to recover, still more spills occurred.

This is no crude, aging municipal system but one of the
nation's modern "super sewer" plants, built with federal funds.
What happened? Changes in the composition of the sewage
during peak wasteloads changed the bacterial balance. Tiny
bacteria used to consume pollutants were smothered by filamen-
tous organisms that clogged the works. The system had to "bypass" sewage into the bay with little or no treatment. Although
the plant spent $150 million more to ensure that the tempera-
mental bacteria received the right amount of air and nutrients,
problems continue today. In 1990, the State Water Resources
Control Board, acting on a petition submitted by Citizens for a
Better Environment, found that the plant discharge still threatens aquatic life. The discharge contributes to the growth of a
bacteria that causes repeat outbreaks of avian botulism, a bird
disease. The discharge has converted a large saltwater marsh,
critical to the survival of endangered species, into a less desirable freshwater marsh. Toxic metals in the discharge pose a
threat to the aquatic food chain. The State Board has directed
the plant to either control these impacts or face penalties and
restrictions on the volume of sewage it can discharge into the
stressed bay. "We are back where we were twenty years ago,"
notes one disgruntled resident.

Some coastal cities build big disposal plants but then forget to
expand and maintain the lines that bring in the raw sewage.
Aging sewer lines clogged with roots and inadequate pump stations contribute to San Diego's infamous rate of sewage spills.
Thanks to more than ninety sewage spills in the past ten years
from collector lines, Mission Bay, a popular recreational area,
has been frequently unusable. In 1989, EPA charged the city

with discharging raw or partially treated sewage into the ocean and local bays on 1,814 occasions since 1983.

Some big plants treat more water than sewage. About 40 percent of the flow that reaches the huge Blue Plains plant in Washington, D.C., consists of storm water that enters sewer lines. EPA estimates that such "infiltration/inflow" contributes 25 percent of the total flow to the nation's plants. This excess flow can lead to more plant overloads and more spills. A rainy day in the Oakland, California, area can trigger sewage overflows at more than 175 locations, thanks to storm water that infiltrates sewer-line joints. These overflows threaten public health, pollute San Francisco Bay, and violate federal laws.

Across the bay from Oakland, San Francisco has spent $700 million to upgrade its leaky sewage system. Yet drizzles can send raw sewage laced with human wastes, toxic chemicals, and waste oil into San Francisco Bay. Like other older cities, San Francisco built a combined sewer system to carry both sewage and storm runoff. Open land was expected to soak up rains. Today, with the land paved over, wet-weather flows quickly overload city plants. The city is building massive tunnels to contain these damaging flows.

Nationwide, there are more than 1,000 combined or partially combined sewer systems. In Boston, combined sewer overflows dump more than five billion gallons of raw sewage into Boston Harbor each year. Along the downtown waterfront, raw sewage gushes out of overflow conduits every day, *even without a rain*. Sewer pipes are too small to carry increased flows from downtown development. Boston can lay claim to one of the country's most polluted bays. Fecal and other organic matter has accumulated to levels of several feet at the bottom of the Inner Harbor. In New York City, some $2 billion in public funds, including sixty-one federal grants, have helped to upgrade the city's fourteen disposal plants. But this investment remains hostage to combined sewers. "When it rains, millions of gallons of untreated sewage are discharged to area waterways, bacteria levels rise precipitously, and beaches have to be closed," reports the General Accounting Office. Even when skies are clear, problems remain. GAO and the New York Public Interest Research Group have found that some city disposal plants repeatedly violate their discharge permits because of "plant inefficiency."

Bans on swimming and on shellfish harvesting become our last defense against sloppy sewage treatment. Harvesting of shellfish—clams, oysters, mussels—has been prohibited or restricted in one-third of the nation's productive waters. In the Gulf of Mexico, nearly 60 percent of the oyster beds are subject to permanent or periodic public health closures, according to Dorothy Leonard, a researcher with the National Oceanic and Atmospheric Administration (NOAA). Despite such bans, the incidence of acute stomach illness among persons eating contaminated shellfish has increased, according to EPA. One health expert—Dr. Herbert DuPont of the University of Texas Health Center—warns that eating raw or partially cooked clams and oysters "is currently a high risk venture at best." Ironically, the bans are an economic boom for outlaw harvesters, who prefer to cash in on America's seafood craze. Illegal poaching has been reported in Rhode Island, New York, Massachusetts, and other coastal states. In a 1990 report to Congress, the National Fish and Wildlife Foundation estimated "that one-fourth of all the molluscan shellfish on the U.S. market have been taken illegally from closed, polluted areas." The sheer size of the closed areas makes enforcement difficult, particularly when outlaw harvesters can afford boats that outrace shellfish patrols. The price of eliminating damaging pollution will be high, but so is the price of tolerating or accepting it, both in terms of our pocketbooks and in terms of our health.

Adequate controls on polluted shellfish are also hampered by policy loopholes. Health officials have relied on "indicator" organisms—coliform bacteria—to indicate the aquatic presence of pathogenic bacteria and viruses. Research by Dr. Victor Cabelli of the University of Rhode Island and by other scientists, however, shows that the pathogenic organisms survive longer in marine waters than the supposed indicator organisms. Shellfish lovers can become ill from consuming clams taken from coastal waters deemed acceptable by current standards.

That brings us to another regulatory shortcoming. EPA and the coastal states issue discharge permits to sewage agencies and industry on a case-by-case, outfall-by-outfall basis without regard to the total wasteloads converging on a particular bay or coastal area. Moreover, discharge permits have focused on "point" sources—industrial and municipal outfalls. Controls on urban and agricultural runoff—the "nonpoint" sources that contribute up to half this nation's pollution load—have been largely voluntary. In other words, our alleged policy to control pollution still fails to reflect how we use our bays and coastal waters as an all-purpose dump. The New York–New Jersey shore—hit by repeated beach closures in the summers of 1987 and 1988— remains hostage to multiple pollution sources: combined sewer overflows, illegal dumping of infectious medical wastes, urban street runoff, sewer plant breakdowns, leaking sewer lines, aerial fallout from smokestacks, river discharges, overflowing landfills, and plastic debris that can ensnare seabirds and marine mammals.

Tired of seeing their beloved Puget Sound victimized by such policy oversights, citizen and community groups in Washington State campaigned to create a public agency able to develop a unified plan to protect and restore the 3,200-square-mile sound. In 1983, the state legislature created the Puget Sound Water Quality Authority. This authority has developed a landmark plan with specific goals, to be implemented by existing state and local agencies. Rather than disappear, the authority remains to track progress and/or the lack thereof. Citizen groups help to monitor water quality and spot possible pollution violations. To cut through the confusing maze of regulatory agencies, a citizen can call one toll-free number to gain information or report problems, from oil spills to washed-up hospital needles. A cigarette tax provides $40 million a year to help fund local pollution control projects. After years of inaction, local governments are beginning to control dairy runoff and septic tank leaks that can turn shellfish beds into health hazards. To fund stormwater-control programs and restore salmon streams, the city of Bellevue taxes property owners for the relative amount of runoff they generate. Larger property owners can detain or recycle stormwater on-site to reduce their taxes.

To the federal Office of Technology Assessment, such "water-body management" is needed to protect our bays and coastal waters from our wasteloads. A joint federal-state effort is under way to clean up Rhode Island's Narragansett Bay, where one-third of the bay is closed to shellfishing. The Save the Bay Association, a citizen group with 10,000 family memberships, monitors compliance with water quality standards and reports on the performance of twenty-nine bayside dischargers. Grease-balls that once saturated swimming areas have decreased. Some shellfish beds have been reopened. Recently, the states bordering Chesapeake Bay agreed to reduce waste nutrients from sewage plants and river discharges by 40 percent by the year 2000.

To meet such critical goals, we must reform our ways of handling wastes on a watery planet. Some communities are learning how to shift away from conventional waterborne disposal. Hike through a pine forest in Clayton County, Georgia, and you may be walking through a waste treatment system. After partial treatment, sewage from 150,000 residents is piped to a storage lagoon where the sludge is separated out; the treated wastewater is then sprayed on 2,725 acres of hilly woodland.

Such "land application" has certain critical advances. The earth contains infinite numbers of tiny organisms that can decompose sewage impurities—and so Clayton County will never have to worry about the nuisance nutrients that sewer authorities spend millions of dollars to remove. Instead, these nutrients help grass and trees grow faster.

"Why pay for something soil and plants will do for free?" asks Wade Nutter, a University of Georgia scientist who helped design the Clayton project. Trees from the irrigated forest are harvested and burned, to dry and pelletize the sludge that is then sold as fertilizer, which helps defray operating expenses. (The operation is possible only because industries must remove certain contaminants from their wastewater before discharging it into the sewer system.) After percolating through the soil, the purified wastewater eventually drains into creeks to help renew the county's drinking supply.

EPA now estimates that such land treatment alternatives, when compared with conventional systems, can cut construction costs by 25 percent and operating costs by 50 percent, depending on the concentration of contaminants and the availability of land.

Today, in virtually every clime across the United States, the "greening" of sewage systems proceeds. Treated sewage from St. Petersburg, Florida, that once polluted Tampa Bay now irrigates 4,400 acres of urban open space, from parks and residential lawns to a golf course. Revenues from water sales help offset operating costs. Tallahassee and Coral Gables have shifted to land application.

California has some 250 reuse projects. The County Sanitation Districts of Los Angeles (CSDLA), which serves four million people, recycles 10 percent of its massive wastewater flow. Treated effluent once wasted to the ocean irrigates campus landscapes and highway medians. Two paper companies use the effluent to process paper pulp. Short of urban space for land application? Part of the reclaimed effluent, which meets applicable health standards, percolates underground to recharge groundwater basins. Sales of this "affluent effluent" help offset treatment costs. Customers save, too; the reclaimed water costs less than imported water supplies. Indeed, such reuse can cut the need to divert more water from watersheds already suffering from low flows. By reducing flows to the agency's large coastal disposal plant, reuse helps forestall plant expansion. As Shakespeare once observed, "The art of our necessities is strange, that can make vile things precious." State regulators have urged the troubled San Jose–Santa Clara sewer plant to shift to reclamation to reduce its damaging bay discharge. California's ongoing drought has served to make reclamation an even more attractive policy option.

After dumping its sewage sludge in the New York Bight for decades, Philadelphia processes it into fertilizer to help reclaim abandoned strip mines and other derelict lands.

Some communities can eliminate the need to escalate to big central plants by improving on a more venerable system. In the septic tank–drainfield system, wastes from a home are piped to an on-site underground tank, where solids settle out. The effluent then flows out into the ground through drains. Each home owner is supposed to keep his or her system in good working order. The many drinking wells and shellfish beds polluted by leaky systems, however, indicate that too many home owners shirk this duty. (Some home owners don't even know where their tanks are located. Others have used buried autos and empty oil drums to serve as septic tanks.)

Faulty septic systems were polluting an ocean lagoon in Stinson Beach, north of San Francisco. A shift to a central sewer system could have eliminated the pollution but would have done so at a cost the 1,800 residents were unprepared to shoulder. Instead, the residents formed a special public district to inspect the 553 individual septic systems. Water service can be cut off to home owners who do not repair defective units. Each home pays $120 a year to fund the district, a fraction of the cost to construct and operate a sewer system.

Even big urban sewage agencies can find cost-effective ways to cope with their massive wasteloads. Rather than make treatment plants bigger, some agencies reduce the excess flows that seep through sewer lines. By repairing seventy-year-old sewer lines, Houston has cut excess flows by thirty-seven million gallons daily and saved $147 million in treatment costs. Does underground sewer repair mean tearing up city streets and angering motorists and streetside merchants? Not anymore. A polyester fiber tubing can be inserted through manholes to reline aging pipes.

Low-flow toilets and shower heads can cut wasteloads, too. The six-gallon toilet flush can be cut to two gallons or less. (A toilet used in Japan gets by with one-half cup per flush.) In California, the Monterey-Carmel area requires low-flow devices in new construction.

Ironically, the shift to broader strategies to control our wasteloads may have been inhibited by the federal sewer grant program. "Federal dominance inadvertently fostered an atmosphere of passive dependency," EPA official Lawrence Jensen has noted. With Uncle Sam willing to subsidize up to 75 percent of the cost to make disposal plants bigger, communities had little incentive to rely on their own resources or ingenuity. "Action on existing needs and planning for future growth was thwarted as some municipalities stood in the federal waiting line for grants," said Jensen. As the Congressional Budget Office reported in 1985, the higher the federal share in sewer plant construction, the more likely the wasteful and inefficient practices—complex treatment programs prone to breakdowns, less rigorous cost controls, oversize capacity, and extended construction schedules.

Risking more sewage overflows and more beach closures while waiting for a federal sewer grant is no longer such a viable strategy. In 1987, Congress decided to replace the federal sewer grants program with a state-run revolving loan program whose monies must be paid back. Those coastal regions which can more effectively manage their wasteloads stand to gain from both an economic and an environmental viewpoint. Those coastal regions which don't should expect to pay a higher price than just more beach closure signs. EPA has been dusting off the enforcement powers that Congress originally gave the agency back in 1972. Since 1984, EPA has filed more than a hundred lawsuits against municipal polluters. In a consent agreement with EPA, the city of Los Angeles agreed to pay a $625,000 fine for illegal spills and discharges that triggered swim bans in Santa Monica Bay. The city also committed itself to build $2 billion worth of sewage improvements or face more fines. Some sewage is being reclaimed to green city parks and a cemetery.

Under state and federal orders, San Diego is patching up another spill-prone system.

Under pressure from federal, state, and private lawsuits—one brought by jogger William Golden on behalf of the city of Quincy—the Boston area is finally cleaning up its sewage act, upgrading its plants with federal, state, and local financing. It may take almost $3 billion and eleven years to render Boston's sewage system safe. Sewer rates are expected to double.

Our bays and coastal waters can no longer serve as a cheap substitute for wise and careful management of our wasteloads. We have come to realize this. We are plugging up some of the worst leaks in our sewage disposal system. But that is not enough. We must deal with all sources of land-based marine pollution or risk jeopardizing our billion-dollar investment in cleanup. In 1990, EPA directed communities to begin the cleanup of their storm-drain flows. And we must not allow the coastal building binge to continue to hook up to sewer systems that are already grossly inadequate. New York City has been approving massive new high-rise complexes augmenting the sewer overflows that can shut down beaches in a three-state area and damage the economy of coastal towns. In 1990, New York state officials were threatening the Big Apple with a sewer hookup ban. California invoked such a ban to get San Diego to upgrade a sewer pump station that was polluting a marine wildlife refuge. A safe sewer system should be a precondition of more development, not an afterthought. The longer it takes us to recognize this, the more Boston Harbors we can expect.

CHAPTER FIFTEEN

The Seaward Migration
of Pollution

It is a modern freighter with an age-old problem. The accumulated trash is dumped overboard into the blue waters of the Gulf of Mexico. While some trash decays, most of the discards remain steadfastly buoyant. They are drawn into lengthy driftlines of flotsam that form a veritable conga line of bobbing trash. Shampoo bottles, plastic flowers, and tampon applicators from cruise ships and egg cartons from navy vessels join the meandering trash parade. So do polystyrene plastic cups and plastic beads that the Mississippi River transports into the Gulf. The 16,000 fishing vessels that harvest the Gulf contribute castaway nets, fish line, and more garbage. The 10,000 workers on the 3,400 oil platforms in the Gulf contribute drums, fuel filters, marker buoys, and more egg cartons. The conga line becomes multilingual, thanks to debris dumped by Japanese, Mexican, Arabian, and Greek shipping crews.

A sea turtle snatching what looks like a jellyfish swallows a plastic bag instead. This lethal look-alike will obstruct the turtle's digestive tract. Death will be slow but sure. The trash line has begun its killing spree. Another turtle ingests so much plastic debris that it becomes too buoyant to dive after real prey. A seabird swallows fish eggs that are actually plastic beads. The seabird feeds this fatal food to its newly hatched chicks. A dolphin entangled on a discarded fish net suffocates. A diving pelican is garroted around the neck by a beverage yoke. The bloated corpses of turtles, seabirds, and dolphins join the silent, strung-out trash line, now more than forty miles long.

A fishing vessel sputters to a halt. Curses wring out over the gulf. The cooling water-intake valves are clogged with plastic sheeting. The sheeting is removed . . . and returned to the lethal driftline of trash.

The currents patiently nudge the trash parade toward one more victim. The waters become more shallow. Swells turn into waves. Item by item, the debris and the dead animals wash up on the white sand beaches of Texas. Texas must spend $14 million a year to keep its shoreline from being buried beneath trash that can last for 450 years. One standard piece of trash costs $1,000 to remove. Because of the toxic risk, unmarked metal drums must be removed by special crews. "We are being swamped by a tidal wave of garbage," says Texas Land Commissioner Garry Mauro. Some seven pounds of buoyant trash wash up daily along each mile of Padre Island National Seashore. By year's end, this seashore can accumulate 673 tons of debris, much of it lightweight plastic. "This is the filthiest national park in the nation," one park ranger has noted. As volunteer trash brigades hand-clean the shore and remove the latest trash load, tankers from Texas refineries depart with more raw material for plants that churn out nearly five billion pounds of raw plastic pellets each year.

The trashing of the Texas shore indicates how our waste-making habits can spread seaward, raise havoc in the open seas, and then return to pummel our already stressed coastal regions. As Texas has learned, controlling an epidemic of open-sea dumping can be a formidable task. The items involved can range from seemingly benign plastic cups to unmarked drums of toxic waste that can endanger beachgoers as well as marine life. The victims of dumping often lack recourse against the careless dumper, if indeed the dumper can even be identified. By being so mobile, seagoing pollution can make a mockery of political accountability.

Like other coastal states, Texas once blamed trashy shores mainly on trashy beachgoers. Signs admonish surfers and fishermen to not litter. Trash cans are deployed. Some signs warn that litterbugs are liable for $50 or $100 fines if caught in the act.

But why were more remote beaches winding up with the most trash? And how can you blame surfers and sport fishermen for such castoff items as toxic waste drums, oil company hard hats, miles of commercial fishnet, and liquor bottles with Dutch labels?

Padre Island is the longest barrier island in the United States. Had real estate developers and revenue officials had their way, it would also have become the longest high-rise resort complex. Instead, the citizens of Texas lobbied Congress to designate much of the island a National Seashore in 1968. This fifty-five-mile-long seashore, with its beaches and natural dunes still intact, hosts about 610,000 people a year, equal to the total that an urban beach stretch along Los Angeles or New Jersey will handle on a long summer weekend. Despite such a light visitor load, Padre Island National Seashore can look like a linear dump.

The seashore's plight stems in part from natural causes. Two longshore currents, one from the southern part of the Gulf, the other from the north, converge on Padre Island, depositing sand, shells, and seaweeds. During the nineteenth century, these converging currents enabled a local rancher to build a home entirely of collected driftwood. Obviously, the currents sweep a wide area. A museum in nearby Corpus Christi exhibits a dugout from the Caribbean region; it had washed up on a local beach.

Couple these converging currents with today's throwaway trash and increased offshore activity and you can understand how Padre Island National Seashore, saved from a destiny of high-rise tourism, must now battle against becoming a coastal capital of trash.

The shore is not the only victim of mobile pollution. In the open sea, fronts develop along the boundaries of water masses that differ in salinity and temperature. Here the surface waters tend to sink, or downwell. This downward motion tends to pull or draw in surrounding flotsam, forming the long driftlines you may see while on a ship or transoceanic flight. To scientists, these driftlines form an important marine habitat. The seaweed and the driftwood provide habitat that small marine organisms can colonize. These tiny animals, in turn, become a food base for juvenile fish and young sea turtles. At the same time, the seaweed can help conceal fish and turtles from tuna and other large predators. Today, the downwelling motion pulls in plastic debris and tar balls as well as floating seaweed. A key linear habitat in the open seas can now carry its own dangers, such as nets that entangle. The mouth and nostrils of sea turtles can be sealed by oil and tar. The turtles may evade the tar balls, only to swallow a plastic bag that clogs their digestive tract.

The proud developers of ubiquitous plastic never anticipated that such values as durability, lightweightness, and relatively cheap cost could, at sea, turn into an environmental horror story. Raw plastic is so cheap to make that there is little incentive to recycle, hence throwaway convenience and more plastics in driftlines and on beaches. The shipping industry dumps about six million metric tons of debris each year, including some 450,000 plastic containers. More is on the way. A major American soup manufacturer is shifting from metal cans to plastics. One plastics industry official claims "almost everything that's in other packaging now is apt to find itself into plastic eventually."

Texas was finding out that throwaway convenience has a price and that Texas, not the dumper, was paying the piper, whether it be beach cleanup or loss of marine resources. Texas had the authority to crack down on a beachside litterbug but not on long-distance dumpers beyond its borders. Researchers concluded that more than 70 percent of the beach trash came from offshore sources and from a downcoast nation, Mexico. Unlike the drift timbers and dugouts of the past, this was trash fit only for dumpsters, landfills, or toxic treatment centers.

To add to its growing frustration, the Lone Star State found out that some federal regulations encourage the use of the open seas as a cost-effective dump. To control entry of foreign pests at our ports, the Department of Agriculture requires that shipboard food wastes be incinerated or steam-sterilized. Rather than comply with these costly port standards, a captain can dump for "free" in the open ocean, beyond the control of coastal states. Who wants to take up valuable pay-cargo space with trash bloated with plastics? Ergo, the seagoing trash parade that can overrun our beaches. Of 73,614 foreign ship landings in the United States in 1986, only 1,731 offloaded any garbage.

It has taken a while, but Texas is learning how to gain the offensive against the trash that desecrates its coast. Offshore oil operators can lose their state oil leases if they ocean-dump solid waste. The offshore oil industry is now educating its work crews on the environmental and economic consequences of plastics dumping. In 1987, Texas teamed up with other concerned coastal states and with environmental groups like the Oceanic Society and the Center for Marine Education to persuade Congress to finally ratify a key annex to the 1973 International Convention for the Prevention of Pollution from Ships (MARPOL). Through this treaty, nations agree to comply with controls on shipboard wastes, including oil and other hazardous wastes. By 1978, annex 5, an optional part of the treaty, was submitted to nation-states for ratification. This annex bans "the disposal into the sea of all plastics, including but not limited to synthetic ropes, synthetic fishing nets and plastic garbage bags." Disposal of nonplastic waste, such as glass and metal, is not permitted within twelve miles of land.

To come into force, annex 5 had to be ratified by nations representing 50 percent of the world's shipping tonnage. A decade later, spurred in part by the plight of Padre Island National

Seashore, the U.S. Congress finally ratified annex 5. By 1988, enough nations had approved ratification to bring annex 5 into force.

Annex 5, by itself, does not mean salvation for trash-stressed shores. At best, it is only a beginning. Plastics continue to kill at sea and wash ashore. To succeed, annex 5 requires extensive public education, provision of adequate port disposal facilities, and enforcement. And then there are the loopholes. Annex 5, like too many international treaties, exempts military vessels. National security presumably would be compromised by submitting to international norms. Yet naval fleets have been among the biggest marine dumpers. Going a step further than annex 5, the U.S. Congress is requiring the U.S. Navy to comply with MARPOL. The navy plans to add trash compactors to its vessels, some of which carry crews of up to 5,000. It is hoped that other naval powers, like Russia, the United Kingdom, and France, will take this step, too. (At one time, there were reports of Soviet naval vessels eagerly picking up trash thrown overboard by U.S. cruisers and aircraft carriers. Thereupon, one U.S. vessel began throwing over countless trash bags, mostly empty, in a pioneer campaign of disinformation by trash.)

How do you get countless recreational boaters and fishermen to respond to annex 5's plastics ban? The Newport, Oregon, fleet of fishermen has spent an average of $2,725 per vessel per year to repair net-fouled props and intakes clogged with plastic sheeting. Recognizing how careless net and plastics disposal can jeopardize their own livelihood, these fishermen committed themselves to port disposal of trash even before annex 5 came into force. "I think any successful fisherman, if he is going to succeed over time, has to be an environmentalist," says Newport fisherman Barry Fisher. Net fragments returned to port are used to repair other nets, as baseball and golf backstops and as temporary cover to help retard hillside erosion. The Newport fishermen have also helped organize an annual marine debris conference that attracts representatives of fishing groups from Japan, China, Canada, and South Korea.

Under annex 5, ports must provide adequate disposal facilities. Ship captains must produce logs showing how solid wastes are handled. In the United States, the Coast Guard is responsible for certifying that major ports comply with disposal requirements. The Coast Guard is also responsible for enforcing the plastics ban within U.S. waters.

What will ports do as more and more vessels unload their plastic wastes? Many plan to truck the accumulated plastic pileups to the nearest landfill or dump, already bloated with landbased plastic wasteloads. Indeed, overflowing landfills can be a major source of trash slicks in some coastal regions. Recently, beaches from New Jersey north to Massachusetts have been contending with an upsurge in hit-and-run trash slicks impregnated with castoff medical needles, blood vials, and surgical tubing. Thanks in part to such handy identifiers as castoff hospital tags, medical bracelets, and prescription bottles, investigators have identified one major tri-state slick source as New York City. The Big Apple uses a fleet of 103 barges to transfer its wasteloads to the world's largest landfill, Fresh Kills on Staten Island. Pesky winds and tides can strip buoyant wastes from the garbage-truck-barge-crane-landfill odyssey that awaits each discarded item of trash. The liberated trash, pushed and prodded by tides and winds, helps form the hit-and-run trash slicks. The Big Apple tells hospitals not to mix medical-related wastes in municipal trash. Rather than pay for local incineration or long-distance hauls to out-of-state waste handlers, some hospitals and medical clinics still persist in dumping and in risking fines.

Such trash slicks show how waste regulations can sometimes serve to transfer, rather than resolve, trash problems. Commercial fishermen who faithfully abide by annex 5 strictures and bring their plastics back to port are greeted by the sight of polystyrene plastic cups from street runoff, landfills, and river discharges floating away on the outgoing tides. According to the Center for Marine Conservation, the bulk of the trash on beaches in southern California is locally generated.

Texas and other coastal states are now trying out other controls on throwaway trash. Eleven coastal states have mandated that six-pack yokes must degrade after a certain duration. Cornstarch can be added to yokes and to plastic shopping bags to hasten degradation. The extent to which degradable plastic will help remains to be seen. Some agents of degradation will work only when exposed to sunlight ("photodegradation"); a partially buried or submerged yoke may still enjoy a long life.

With their landfills and their beaches overflowing with trash, eastern states like New Jersey and Rhode Island have mandated recycling at the municipal level. Here up to 20 percent of the solid waste stream, including plastic containers, are now being diverted into recycling programs. Instead of choking a seabird, plastics can be recycled as traffic cones. By 1989, stung in part by publicity from its wide-ranging trash slicks, New York City even adopted a mandatory recycling law.

Unlike the demand for recycled aluminum, the demand for recycled plastics is in its infancy. Toxic residues in plastic containers can limit recycling options. Some plastics manufacturers, however, appear ready to step up recycling programs; they prefer recycling to degradation, which can impinge on the shelf life of plastic. On such market considerations ride the future condition of beaches and driftlines.

Professor Tony Amos of the University of Texas Marine Science Center at Port Aransas conducted many of the early beach surveys that made Texas officials aware of the causes behind the trashed shores. He still gets up early in the morning to see what the tides have brought to Mustang Island and Padre Island. Today, he is trying to divine how successfully the emerging controls on marine dumping are working. He has seen a drop in oil production debris. "But I don't know if this is because of the new controls, or the recent recession in the oil industry. Maybe it's a bit of both," he notes.

While heartened by the annex 5 ban on plastics, Texas still does not like those provisions that permit dumping of nonplastic wastes within twelve miles of shore. It has learned all too well how currents can supersede such mileage limits on dumping. Annex 5 does have a provision in which semienclosed seas can be designated "special areas," where no dumping is permitted. The Black, Red, Baltic, and Mediterranean seas have been so designated. In 1990, the International Maritime Organization initiated a procedure to so designate the Gulf of Mexico. The designation may extend to the Caribbean; island nations there don't want marine dumpers to substitute their waters for Gulf waters.

Coastal nations of Africa must already contend with the shifting nature of another type of dumping. In 1988, after a number of European firms were found to be shipping toxic wastes to impromptu dumps in Nigeria, Ghana, and other nations, the United Nations Environmental Program helped develop an international treaty intended to control such practices. Toxic waste firms must notify their governments that they have received permission from a "host" nation prior to shipping toxic wastes. A total ban on such toxic exports was rejected. Some African nations wanted to have the option of shipping their own toxic wastes to Europe for treatment. Other nations wanted to have the option of receiving income from the siting of toxic dumps. Today, Togo and other small African nations are using their admittedly limited naval patrols to board vessels passing through their coastal waters to check for the presence of toxic waste drums. With restrictions on on-land disposal, these nations are concerned that dumpers may simply push drums overboard and not worry about obtaining permits from anybody.

Given our waste-making proclivities, the problem of marine dumping could be with us for some time. The industrial nations of the world, responsible for generating most of the throwaway trash and the toxic drums, were slow to ratify such necessary measures as annex 5 or to set up "cradle-to-the-grave" tracking systems for toxic wastes. The Texas coast had to be buried in trash before Congress acted on annex 5. Now Congress is stinting on funds that would enable the Coast Guard to effectively enforce its provisions. If public education and current regulations are not sufficient to control mobile trash, more attention must be paid to dealing with the problem at its source. For too long, our oceans have been at the mercy of market decisions that ignore or overlook the ultimate fate of the products we use. The sooner we can learn to recycle and reduce our waste streams, the safer our seas will be.

Amends for a
Blue World

Two decades ago, the marine environment was being touted as a resource bonanza to prolong industrial affluence and bootstrap the Third World into prosperity. Today, the "blue frontier" can be a crowded and stressed environment where beach closures, shellfish harvest bans, and seafood warnings become routine management tools. At last count, coastal states in the United States had issued over fifty health advisories against consumption of finfish contaminated by toxic chemicals, from white croaker off Los Angeles to striped bass off New York coastal waters. In a world being overtaken by its own waste-making proclivities, closures rather than cleanups can become the chosen management tool. Our shores and seas can turn into what accountants would call "nonperforming assets."

Or even worse, dangerous and deadly liabilities. Our traditional eagerness to urbanize the active beach zone means that more billion-dollar urban disasters are inevitable. By regarding landforms as dynamic as beaches and deltas are as mere real estate, we have invited catastrophe.

Our belief in the ocean as a fish bonanza has caused nations to build fishing fleets well beyond the capacity of more and more stocks to sustain such frenetic effort. Ergo, too many fishermen, not enough fish. This is the sort of human predicament that grandiose marine expectations can foster.

The desperate quest by developing nations for economic survival can accelerate such degradation. The ministates of the Caribbean have gone into debt to reduplicate such disaster-prone resorts on their own slim shores. Offshore, the quest to make the seas pay results in more backlashes. Coral reefs in the Philippines sustain beautiful rainbow-hued fish. Fishermen harvest these tropical fish to supply the demand for eye-catching fish so that aquarium owners in Europe and North America can impress their guests and their clients. To capture fish faster, fishermen stun them with squirts of cyanide. But the cyanide is toxic to the very reefs that support fish, edible and hobby. Meanwhile, the cyanide-stunned fish tend to die sooner in aquarium captivity, thus accelerating the demand for more cyanide harvests . . . and more crippled reefs. Tropical fish brokers often supply cyanide to the fishermen. It is easy to be critical of such a shortsighted practice. But the developing nations need economic alternatives, not calls for economic abstinence. And it is the industrial nations that engage in the race to capture major marine stocks to sustain our current seafood celebration.

The style of governance that has evolved on this planet clearly abets such predicaments. Each and every nation retains the right, if not always the capability, to deplete fish stocks and alter marine ecosystems regardless of how wide-ranging the effects. International conventions attempt to control ocean dumping and vessel pollution but not the major source of marine pollution— land-based sources like sewer outfalls and river discharges laden with excess nutrients and floatable debris. We still consider national security in terms of territorial rights, national borders, missiles, and standing armies. Yet the most basic form of national security—a healthy biosphere—can be left to political chance.

Clearly, the marine environment is being overtaken by the

"deplete and move on" frontier mind-set that has laid waste to too much of our land. It need not be that way. We are learning, albeit slowly, that we can reverse, not just slow down, such degradation. After decades of being filled in and buried beneath fill, San Francisco Bay is "growing" at the average rate of seventy acres a year. Diked tidelands are reopened to the tides and schooling fish. Old pastures are restored as freshwater wetlands. These projects make for a safer coast as well. Urbanize these lowlands and you risk predictable earthquake and flooding hazards. We can have more Hilos, not less, along the shore.

By learning to recycle and reduce our wasteloads, we are finding a more permanent means of protecting and restoring marine water quality. By reclaiming sewage, coastal cities can reduce marine pollution and the demand to divert more water from other watersheds. By turning to fuel-efficient cars and renewable energy, coastal regions can reduce the need for and the risks from marine oil development. Thus, the goal of a restored shore and a protected sea can finally induce us to re-form the wasteful resource practices that result in the deplete-and-move-on mind-set.

The way we govern our water bodies can frustrate such perspectives. According to the Environmental Protection Agency (EPA), the sheer number of public agencies involved in coastal and marine matters (more than thirty at the federal level alone) can result in "reactive programs with few integrated goals for managing the near coastal environment." At times, the federal coastal presence can resemble the Keystone Kops. The federal Bureau of Reclamation has promoted water diversion projects that the National Oceanic and Atmospheric Administration claims can alter vital river inflows to our bays, deltas, and estuaries. The Office of Management and Budget can push for more offshore oil leases, which the EPA and coastal states consider too great a risk to coastal ecosystems.

Today, as in Puget Sound and Chesapeake Bay, regional bodies that can treat a bay as one entity rather than a piecemeal resource are emerging. EPA's National Estuary Program helps fund these efforts. Eventually such bodies may have the political clout to prevent the watershed abuses that counter gains in better coastal sewage treatment and wetland protection. And they may help overturn the federal water subsidies that take away river inflows needed by our deltas and bays. As coastal regions respond to the marine challenge, the federal government has the opportunity to develop a national coastal protection and restoration program. In 1991, Senator Bill Bradley (D.–N.J.) and Congressman George Miller (D.–Ca.9) were pushing for reforms that would phase out the federal water subsidies that place fish and bay ecosystems at the mercy of cotton and rice farmers. Instead of rebuilding storm-prone coastal communities for another collision with hurricanes, the Federal Emergency Management Agency can help fund coastal restoration projects that reduce such risks.

Given the expanding challenge of the marine environment, there is a greater need to develop scientific and technical resources, along with sound policy. In 1990, Congress passed a bill pushed by Senator George Mitchell (D.–Maine) and Congressman Garry Studds (D.–Ma.) that creates eight regional marine-science research centers. One priority: better monitoring of the marine environment to anticipate problems and improve accountability over current cleanup and protection programs. In 1990 the National Research Council reported that current monitoring efforts are often too fragmented and narrow in scope to ensure that waters are always safe to swim in, seafood is safe to eat, and the marine ecosystem is being effectively protected. Regional monitoring systems could help tell us the degree to which natural forces and man-made activities are responsible for changes in the marine environment. Given the fact we must spend billions, we need a system that can tell us if we are doing the job.

More scientific resources are needed to improve and refine restoration efforts. Resource agencies may permit a developer to create artificial wetlands to replace natural wetlands converted to building sites. Just "greening up" the nearest available open space with transplanted marsh plants or mangrove trees, however, is rarely adequate replacement for a natural marsh whose biodiversity has evolved over the decades, according to Dr. Joy Zedler, a wetland scientist at San Diego State University.

In the Mediterranean, nations split by ancient differences in politics, language, and religion are participating in a joint convention to restore the sea on which they once fought their battles. For the Mediterranean nations, a healthier sea is a prerequisite for retaining a critical component. Coastal tourism provides far more income to these nations than marine oil development or industrial fishing.

The Mediterranean initiative, vigorously supported by the United Nations Environmental Program, suggests how regional frameworks can transcend national marine borders. The United Nations Regional Seas Program has expanded to eight other areas, including the Caribbean, the South Pacific, and West Africa. The Caribbean basin is crisscrossed by extensive tanker transits to and from U.S. ports. One massive, encircling oil spill could bankrupt the marginal economy of a small nation in the basin. The United States, one of twenty-five nations in the Caribbean program, has helped support a regional spill response system that, it is hoped, will learn from the *Exxon Valdez* spill. These nations could also benefit from U.S. experience in assessing and recovering costs for spill damages and in restoring wetlands and mangrove forests.

Some environmental threats must be addressed at a global level. Here Grotius's concept of a global commons can have renewed meaning. The United Nations effort to control the destructive impact of high-seas drift nets is one example of how global action can begin to confront reckless fishing practices beyond state jurisdiction. The International Whaling Commission has the opportunity to make comebacks like that of the gray whale the rule rather than the exception. Another UNEP program, the Global Environment Monitoring System (GEMS), is working to expand monitoring technology into remote locations and into developing nations so we gain a more accurate picture of the changing condition of the Watery Planet.

If the greenhouse effect and global warming take hold, low-lying coastal regions, including entire island nations like the Maldives in the Indian Ocean, will face a submarine existence as sea levels rise. In 1992, the United Nations Conference on Conservation and Development will be considering controls on the cause of global warming—fossil fuel emissions. Given the economic stakes involved, this conference will be a real test for nations to forgo short-term economic benefits for long-term stability.

The emerging ability of coastal regions to shift to more efficient energy use, land use, water use, and waste reduction takes on added significance. The more we can transfer such technology to developing nations, the more prepared they will be to merge development needs with environmental goals. The more industrial nations can reduce or eliminate toxic wastes, the less incentive, legal or illegal, to export such wastes overseas. The more we can develop a sense of mutual security on a watery planet, the more we can redirect resources to critical needs. Does it make sense for the United States to spend billions to make our nuclear subs quieter and less detectable while stinting on energy initiatives to forestall the greenhouse effect and the gradual drowning of coastal lowlands, including naval stations?

Environmental groups, fraternal organizations, and other nongovernmental agencies are playing a key role in fostering such a sense of mutual security. An environmental group, Greenpeace, helped alert nations in West Africa to illegal and unauthorized dumping of toxic wastes from Europe. The South Coast Rotary Club in Costa Mesa, California, has provided money and equipment to help Mexican coastal communities build water treatment facilities. There can be "sister bay" alliances in which advocacy groups for urban bays in the United States can trade experiences and ideas with their counterparts in South America, Asia, and Eastern Europe. Perhaps such an alliance can foster a transborder effort to restore part of the Colorado River delta in Mexico, made dry, salty, and pollution-prone by too many dams and diversion projects on the U.S. side of the border.

The ultimate challenge of the ocean is clear. It is political. What is "conquered" by technology must be governed. The community of nations must respond to this challenge; the pervasive character of the ocean will permit no less. The incentives for rational planning and use are becoming more apparent. But the obstacles remain: the historic frontier mind-set of deplete-and-move-on, even as we run out of virgin frontiers.

Through time, we have expressed a universal affection and respect for shore and sea, as reflected in the works of Byron, Cicero, Debussy, Winslow Homer, Conrad, Melville, and the millions who walk daily along the ocean rim. This affection and appreciation has never been tested for its true depth and strength. Only recently have the oceans needed our care. Now they belong to us, to do with as we choose. It behooves us now and then to read Byron, view Homer, and listen to Debussy. Their shores and seas should not be forgotten.

Sources

CHAPTER ONE.   SEAWEED: THE OCEAN'S UNSUNG GIFT

16 Boalch, Gerald. 1981. Do we really need to grow macro-
    cystis in Europe? *Xth International Seaweed Symposium* (Ber-
    lin: Walter Gruyter & Co.), 663.

CHAPTER TWO.   ARE WE FISHING TOO FAR DOWN THE
                FOOD CHAIN?

28 National Fish and Wildlife Foundation. 1990. *Needs As-
    sessment of the National Marine Fisheries Service* (Washing-
    ton, D.C.), 50.
29 Folke, Carl and Nils Kautsky. 1989. The role of ecosystems
    for a sustainable development of aquaculture. *Ambio*
    18:242.

CHAPTER THREE.   LEAVING ROOM FOR WHALES

38 Scammon, Charles. 1874. *The Marine Mammals of the
    North-Western Coast of North America* (San Francisco: John
    H. Carmany Co.; from the 1968 reprint by Dover Publish-
    ers), 263.
40 Gilmore, R. M. 1960. A census of the California gray
    whale. In *Scientific Fisheries Report No. 342* (Washington,
    D.C.: U.S. Fish and Wildlife Service), 1–30.
41 Fowler, Gene. 1944. *Good Night, Sweet Prince* (New York:
    Viking Press), 256.
43 Rohter, Larry. 1988. Dangers await gray whales on return
    to winter home. *New York Times* Dec. 20. III, 4:1.

44 Scott, Janny. 1987. Interaction of gray whales, boats studied. *Los Angeles Times* Nov. 29, p. 19.
45 Fritsch, Jane. 1989. Panel refuses Japan's whaling request. *Los Angeles Times* June 17. I, 33:1.

CHAPTER FOUR.   SECOND CHANCE FOR WILD SALMON

53 California Advisory Committee on Salmon and Steelhead Trout. 1988. *Restoring The Balance* Annual report (Sausalito, Calif.), 37.
54 National Park Service. 1987. *Tenth Annual Report to Congress on the Status of Implementation of the Redwood National Park* (Redwood National Park, Crescent City, Calif.), 26.

CHAPTER FIVE.   BOUNDARIES FOR A BOUNDLESS OCEAN

62 Grotius, Hugo. 1604. *Commentary on the Law of Prize and Booty.* From the 1950 translation by Clarendon Press (Oxford), chapter 12.
66 Fulton, Thomas. 1911. *The Sovereignty of the Sea* (Edinburgh: Blackwood), 575.
66 McDougal, Myres, and William Burke. 1962. *Public Order of the Oceans* (New Haven: Yale Press).

CHAPTER SEVEN.   STAKING OUT THE DEEP SEABED

80 Mero, John. 1965. *The Mineral Resources of the Sea* (Amsterdam: Elsevier), 280, 279.
87 National Oceanic and Atmospheric Administration. 1989. *Deep seabed mining,* report to Congress (Washington, D.C.), 4.
87 United Nations Environment Program (UNEP). 1990. *The state of the marine environment,* UNEP Regional Seas Reports and Studies No. 115 (New York, N.Y.), 101.
89 National Academy of Sciences. 1987. *Technology Requirements for Assessment and Development of Hard Mineral Resources in the U.S. Exclusive Economic Zone* (Washington, D.C.), 104.

CHAPTER EIGHT. **BLINDERS FOR THE OCEAN**

93 Burke, William. 1970. *Marine Science Research and International Law*, Occasional Paper #8 (Providence: Law of the Sea Institute, University of Rhode Island).

95–96 Ross, David. 1986. Ocean science: Its place in the new order of the oceans. In *The New Order of the Oceans*, G. Pontecorvo. ed. (New York: Columbia University Press), 83.

CHAPTER ELEVEN. **DELTAS IN DISTRESS**

122 House Committee on Merchant Marine and Fisheries. 1989. Hearings on a bill to expand the Coastal Barrier Resources System. Serial No. 101–35. Testimony by Dr. Robert C. Sheets. p. 21.

CHAPTER TWELVE. **THE LONG, STICKY REACH OF OIL**

132 Johnston, Kathy. 1990. Is our future rigged? *New Times* (San Luis Obispo, Calif.), August 30. 12.

143 Smith, Gordon W. 1990. The fight for a restored wetland in Huntington Beach. *Coast & Ocean* 6(2): 45.

CHAPTER THIRTEEN. **SEAS OF SLIME, SEAS OF DEATH**

147 Anderson, Donald. 1989. Toxic algal blooms and red tides: A global perspective. In *Red Tides: Biology, Environmental Science, and Toxicology*, T. Okaichi, et al., eds. (New York: Elsevier), 12.

147 Ibid., 13.

148 Morton, Brian. 1989. Hong Kong's pigs in the sea. In *Marine Pollution Bulletin* May. 200.

148 Cherfis, Jeremy. 1990. The fringe of the ocean—Under siege from land. *Science* 248:163.

149 Anderson, Toxic algal blooms, 15.

CHAPTER FOURTEEN.   SWAMPED BY SEWAGE

156 National Fish and Wildlife Foundation. 1990. *Needs Assessment of the National Marine Fisheries Service* (Washington, D.C.).

Select Bibliography

CHAPTER ONE.   SEAWEED: THE OCEAN'S UNSUNG GIFT

Abbott, Isabella, and Eleanor H. Williamson. 1974. *Limu*. Lawai, Kauai, Hawaii: Pacific Tropical Botanical Garden.

Abbott, Isabella, Michael S. Foster, and Louise F. Eklund. 1980. *Pacific Seaweed Aquaculture*. La Jolla, Calif.: California Sea Grant College Program.

Dixon, Peter. 1977. *Biology of the Rhodophyta*. Otto Koeltz Science Publishers, Koenigstein, Germany.

Doty, Maxwell. 1981. *The Diversified Farming of Coral Reefs*. Honolulu: University of Hawaii Press.

Foster, M. S., and D. R. Schiel. 1985. *The Ecology of Giant Kelp Forests in California*. Biological Report 85(7.2). Slidell, La.: U.S. Department of Interior, Fish and Wildlife Service, National Coastal Ecosystems Team.

Marine Review Committee. 1989. *Final Report on the Effects of San Onofre Nuclear Generating Station*. MRC Document No. 89-02. Report prepared for California Coastal Commission, San Francisco.

McPeak, Ron, and Dale Glantz. 1984. Harvesting California's kelp forests. *Oceanus* 27(1).

Moss, James R., and Maxwell Doty. 1987. *Establishing a Seaweed Industry in Hawaii*. Study prepared for Aquaculture Development Program, Hawaii Department of Land and Natural Resources, Honolulu.

Neushul, Michael. 1978. Domestication of the giant kelp, macrocystis, as a marine plant biomass producer. In *The Marine Plant Biomass of the Pacific Northwest Coast*. Corvallis, Oreg.: Oregon State University.

North, W. J. 1971. The biology of giant kelp beds in California. *Nova Hedwigia*:32.

Scofield, W. L. 1959. History of kelp harvesting in California. *California Fish and Game* 45:135–57.

Washington State Department of Natural Resources. 1987. *Final Environmental Impact Statement: Nori Farming and Processing in Washington State*. Olympia, Wash.

CHAPTER TWO.   ARE WE FISHING TOO FAR DOWN THE FOOD CHAIN?

Antarctic and Southern Ocean Coalition. 1991. *Report prepared by Evelyn Hurwich on the 1990 Antarctic Treaty Special Consultative Meeting on the Antarctic Environment*. Washington, D.C.

Glantz, M. H., ed. 1980. *Resource Management and Environmental Uncertainty*. New York: John Wiley & Sons.

Marks, Beth. 1991. *Report to Alliance for Antarctica on Ninth Meeting of the Convention for the Conservation of Antarctic Marine Living Resources*. Sierra Club, Washington, D.C.

McEvoy, A. 1986. *The Fisherman's Problem: Ecology and Law in the California Fisheries*. New York: Cambridge University Press.

McEvoy, A., and H. N. Scheiber. 1984. Scientists, entrepreneurs, and the policy process: a study of the post-1945 California sardine depletion. *Journal of Economic History* 44:393–413.

National Marine Fisheries Service. 1989. *Status of the Fishery Resources off the Northeastern United States for 1989*. Woods Hole, Mass.

Radovich, J. 1982. The collapse of the California sardine fishery. *California Cooperative Oceanic Fisheries Investigation Report* 23:56–78.

Thomson, Cynthia. 1990. The market for fish meal and oil in the United States: 1960–1988 and future prospects. *California Cooperative Oceanic Fisheries Investigation Report* 31:124–31.

World Resources Institute. 1990. Focus on Antarctica. In *World Resources 1990–91*. Washington, D.C.

CHAPTER THREE.   LEAVING ROOM FOR WHALES

Brownell, Robert L., Jr., Katherine Ralls, and William F. Perrin. 1989. The plight of the forgotten whales. *Oceanus* 32 (1):5–11.

Jones, Mary Lou, Steven Swartz, and Stephen Leatherwood, eds. 1989. *The Gray Whale*. Orlando, Fla.: Academic Press.

Marine Mammal Commission. 1988–1990. *Annual Reports*. Washington, D.C.

Marx, Wesley. 1988. Vanishing Vaquitas. Oceans 21:5.

CHAPTER FOUR.   SECOND CHANCE FOR WILD SALMON

California Sea Grant College Program. n.d. *California's Salmon Resource*. La Jolla, Calif.

Carnes, Todi S. 1990. Federal reserved water rights and the Everglades National Park. *Florida Bar Journal* 60:4.

National Park Service. 1987. *An Evaluation of Experimental Rehabilitation Work in Redwood National Park*. Redwood National Park, Arcata, Calif.

Schrepfer, Susan. 1983. *The Fight to Save the Redwoods*. Madison, Wis.: University of Wisconsin Press.

U.S. Department of Justice. 1990. Comments of the United States on the draft SWIM plan for the Everglades. Dated Feb. 28, and addressed to the South Florida Water Management District. Prepared by department's Land and Natural Resources Division, Washington, D.C.

CHAPTER FIVE.   BOUNDARIES FOR A BOUNDLESS OCEAN

Corbett, P. E. 1951. *Law and Society in the Relations of States*. New York: Harcourt, Brace and Co.

Jessup, Philip. 1948. *A Modern Law of Nations*. New York: Macmillan.

Knight, W. S. M. 1932. *The Life and Works of Hugo Grotius*. London: Sweet and Maxwell.

Reiff, Henry. 1959. *The United States and the Treaty Law of the Sea*. Minneapolis: University of Minnesota.

CHAPTER SIX.   THE WANDERING TUNA: IN SEARCH OF
                                STEWARDS

Cicin-Sain, Biliana, Michael K. Orbach, and Jorge A. Vargas. 1983. U.S. Mexican parley debates relations on marine resources. *Oceanus* 26:4.

Doulman, David J. 1987. *Tuna Issues and Perspectives in the Pacific Islands Region.* Honolulu: East-West Center.

Holing, Dwight. 1986. The tuna-porpoise issue resurfaces. *Pacific Discovery* 39:3.

Joseph, James. 1987. The aquatic resources of the Pacific: Their conservation and management. Address to the XVI Pacific Science Congress in Seoul, Korea.

Joseph, James, Witold Klawe, and Pat Murphy. 1988. *Tuna and Billfish—Fish without a Country.* La Jolla, Calif.: Inter-American Tropical Tuna Commission.

Marine Mammal Commission. 1988–1990. *Annual Reports.* Washington, D.C.

CHAPTER SEVEN.   STAKING OUT THE DEEP SEABED

Broadus, J. M. 1986. Asian Pacific marine minerals and industry structure. *Marine Resource Economics* 3:1.

Buzan, Berry. 1976. *Seabed Politics.* New York: Praeger.

California Department of Justice. 1984. Comments on draft environmental impact statement on proposed polymetallic sulfide minerals lease offering, Gorda Ridge area offshore Oregon and Northern California. Dated March 15, and addressed to U.S. Minerals Management Service.

Curtis, Clifton. 1983. The environmental aspects of deep ocean mining. *Oceanus* 25:3.

General Accounting Office. 1983. *Uncertainties Surround Future of U.S. Ocean Mining.* Report to Congress. Washington, D.C.

Minerals Management Service. 1983. Draft environmental impact statement for proposed polymetallic sulfide minerals leasing offering on Gorda Ridge. Washington, D.C.

Wijkman, Per Magnus. 1982. UNCLOS and the redistribution of ocean wealth. *Journal of World Trade* 16:1.

CHAPTER EIGHT.   BLINDERS FOR THE OCEAN

Brown, E. D., and R. R. Churchill. 1987. *The UN Convention on the Law of the Sea: Impact and Implementation.* Honolulu: Law of the Sea Institute, University of Hawaii.

Deacon, Margaret. 1971. *Scientists of the Sea, 1650–1900: A Study of Marine Science.* New York: Academic Press.

Herdman, William. 1923. *Founders of Oceanography.* London: Edward Arnold.

Intergovernmental Oceanographic Commission. 1985. *Marine Sciences and Ocean Services for Development.* United Nations Educational, Scientific and Cultural Organization (UNESCO), Paris.

Keller, G. H., and D. B. Prior. 1986. Sediment dynamics of the Huanghe (Yellow River) Delta and neighboring Gulf of Bohai, People's Republic of China: Projected overview. *Geo-Marine Letters* 6:63–66.

Murray, John, ed. 1885. *Report of the Scientific Results of the Voyage of H.M.S. Challenger.* London.

———. 1913. *The Ocean.* London: Williams and Norgate, Ltd.

Palacio, Francisco. 1977. *Towards a Marine Policy in Latin America.* Woods Hole, Mass.: Woods Hole Oceanographic Institute.

U.S. State Department. *1987 and 1988 Research Clearance Summaries.* Prepared by W. Thomas Cocke, research vessel clearance officer, Office of Ocean Affairs, Washington, D.C.

CHAPTER NINE.   THE DROWNING OF THE SANDY SHORE

Bascom, Willard. 1964. *Waves and Beaches.* New York: Anchor Books.

Bush, David M., ed. 1990. *Recovering from Hugo: Preparing for Hilda.* Durham, N.C.: Program for the Study of Developed Shorelines, Duke University Department of Geology.

Clark, John. 1977. *The Beaches of Oahu.* Honolulu: University of Hawaii Press.

Federal Emergency Management Agency. 1989. *Hurricane Hugo.* A report by the Interagency Hazard Mitigation Team. Region 4, Atlanta.

Federal Insurance Administration. 1990. *Summary and Assessment of National Flood Insurance Program Repetitive Loss Data.* Office of Loss Reduction, Washington, D.C.

Godschalk, David R., David Brower, and Timothy Beatley. 1989. *Catastrophic Coastal Storms.* Durham, N.C.: Duke University Press.

Miller, H. Crane. 1990. *Hurricane Hugo: Learning from South Carolina.* Report to Office of Ocean and Coastal Resources Management, National Oceanic and Atmospheric Administration, Washington, D.C.

National Oceanic and Atmospheric Administration. 1990. *Coastal Management Solutions to Natural Hazards.* Office of Ocean and Coastal Resource Management, Washington, D.C.

National Research Council. 1987. *Responding to Changes in Sea Level: Engineering Implications.* Washington, D.C.: National Academy Press.

Pilkey, Orrin H., Sr., et al. 1983. *Coastal Design.* New York: Van Nostrand Reinhold.

Platt, Rutherford, Shelia Pelczarski, and Barbara Burbank, eds. 1987. *Cities on the Beach: Management Issues of Developed Coastal Barriers.* Chicago: University of Chicago.

CHAPTER TEN.   LIVING WITH KILLER WAVES

Belt, Robert M. 1974. Letter to author, March 20.

Federal Emergency Management Agency. 1990. *Hazard Mitigation Opportunities for California.* Report by the state/federal hazard mitigation survey team for the Loma Prieta earthquake October 17, 1989. Washington, D.C.

Fukuda, Robert. 1974. Letter to author, March 27.

General Accounting Office. 1969. *Federal Disaster Assistance to State and Local Governments.* Washington, D.C.

Hawaii Redevelopment Agency. 1965. *Urban Renewal Plan.* County of Hawaii, Hilo.

CHAPTER ELEVEN.   DELTAS IN DISTRESS

Boesch, D. F. 1987. Louisiana estuaries: Issues, resources, status and management. In *Coastal Zone 1987*, Washington, D.C.: Coastal Society.

Boesch, D. F., D. Levin, D. Nummedal, and K. Bowles. 1983. *Subsidence in Coastal Louisiana.* Washington, D.C.: U.S. Fish and Wildlife Service.

Coalition to Restore Coastal Louisiana. 1989. *Coastal Louisiana: Here Today, Gone Tomorrow?* Baton Rouge, La.

Crawford, K. C. 1979. Hurricane surge potential over southeast Louisiana as revealed by a storm-surge forecast model: A preliminary study. *Bulletin of the American Meteorological Society* 60(5).

Davis, D. W., James McCloy, and Alan Craig. 1987. Man's response to coastal change in the northern Gulf of Mexico. *Resource Management and Optimization* 5 (1–4): 257–97.

Day, J. W., and P. H. Templet. 1989. Consequences of sea level rise: Implications from the Mississippi Delta. *Coastal Management* 17:241–57.

Environmental Protection Agency. 1987. *Saving Louisiana's Coastal Wetlands.* Prepared by the Louisiana Wetland Protection Panel. Washington, D.C.

Federal Emergency Management Agency. 1986. Interagency Post-Flood Recovery Progress Report for Nov. 1, 1985 disaster declaration in State of Louisiana. FEMA-752-Dr. Washington D.C.

Gagliano, S. W. 1981. *Special Report on Marsh Deterioration and Land Loss in the Deltaic Plain of Coastal Louisiana.* Baton Rouge, La.: Coastal Environments.

Louisiana Wetland Conservation and Restoration Task Force. 1990. *Coastal Wetlands Conservation and Restoration Plan.* Baton Rouge, La.

Micklin, Philip P. 1985. The diversion of Soviet rivers. *Environment* 27(2).

———. 1988. Desiccation of the Aral Sea: A water management disaster in the Soviet Union. *Science* 241:1170–76.

Miller, Taylor, Gary Weatherford, and John Thorson. 1986. *The Salty Colorado.* Washington, D.C.: Conservation Foundation; Napa, Calif.: John Muir Institute.

National Weather Service. 1980. *Use of a Hurricane Storm-Surge Forecast Model for Southeast Louisiana.* National Oceanic and Atmospheric Administration Technical Memorandum NWS SR-102. Washington, D.C.

Rosengurt, M. A., M. J. Herz, and S. Feld. 1987. The role of water diversions in the decline of fisheries of the Delta-San Francisco Bay ecosystem (1921–1983). Technical Report No. 87-8. Tiburon, Calif.: Paul Romberg Tiburon Center for Environmental Studies, San Francisco State University.

Rosengurt, M. A., and Joel Hedgpeth. 1989. The impact of altered flow on the ecosystem of the Caspian Sea. *Aquatic Sciences* 1(2).

CHAPTER TWELVE.   THE LONG, STICKY REACH OF OIL

Chevron USA Inc. 1983. Letter to California Coastal Commission regarding Point Arguello permit, dated Nov. 4. Signed by Clair Ghylin, General Manager—Land, Western Region.

Cicin-Sain, Biliana. 1986. Offshore oil development in California: Challenges to governments and to the public interest. *Public Affairs Report* (Institute of Governmental Studies, University of California at Berkeley) 27 (1–2).

Golden, Frederic, ed. 1989. Special issue on the oceans and global warming. *Oceanus* 32(2).

Hershman, Marc J., et al. 1988. *State and Local Influence over Offshore Oil Decisions*. Seattle: University of Washington Sea Grant Program.

Marx, Wesley. 1971. *Oilspill*. San Francisco: Sierra Club.

———. 1983. An offshore battleground. *California Journal* 15(9).

National Research Council. 1989. *The Adequacy of Environmental Information for Outer Continental Shelf Oil and Gas Decisions: Florida and California*. Washington, D.C.: National Academy Press.

Natural Resources Defense Council. 1990. *No Safe Harbor: Tanker Safety in America's Ports*. New York.

Office of Technology Assessment. 1990. *Coping with an Oiled Sea*. Washington, D.C.

Santa Barbara County. 1990. Letter to R. Spier, Department of Energy, dated Aug. 9. Signed by John Patton, Director, County Energy Division.

———. 1990. Letter to Admiral James Watkins, Secretary of Energy, regarding Point Arguello project, dated Aug. 14. Signed by Thomas Rogers, Chairman of the County Board of Supervisors.

United States District Court for the Northern District of California. 1990. Consent decree and appendix for United States of America v. Shell Oil Company. Filed March 26.

World Resources Institute. 1990. Climate change: A global concern and energy sections. In *World Resources 1990–91*. New York: Oxford University Press.

CHAPTER THIRTEEN.   SEAS OF SLIME, SEAS OF DEATH

Chang, J., and E. J. Carpenter. 1985. Blooms of the dinoflagellate *Gyrodinium aureolum* in a Long Island estuary. *Marine Biology* 89:83–93.

Environmental Defense Fund. 1988. *Polluted Coastal Waters: The Role of Acid Rain*. Prepared by Diane Fisher, Jane Ceraso, Thomas Mathew, and Michael Oppenheimer. New York.

Gutis, Philip. 1988. Troubled seas: Global red tides of algae bring new fears. *New York Times* May 3.

Larsson, Ulf, Ragnar Elmgren, and Fredrik Wulff. 1985. *Eutrophication and the Baltic Sea: Causes and consequences. Ambio* 14(1).

Murakawa, Masamichi. 1987. Marine pollution and countermeasures in Japan. *Oceanus* 30(1).

Nishitani, Louisa, and Kenneth Chew. 1986. *Gathering Safe Shellfish in Washington*. Advisory Report, University of Washington Sea Grant Program, Seattle.

Okaichi, Tomotoshi, Donald Anderson, and Takahis Nemoto, eds. 1987. *Red Tides: Biology, Environmental Science, and Toxicology*. New York: Elsevier.

Shumway, Sandra. 1988. Toxic algal blooms: Hazards to shellfish and industry. *Journal of Shellfish Research* 7(4).

Steidinger, Karen, and Edwin Joyce, Jr. 1973. *Florida Red Tides*. Educational Series No. 17. St. Petersburg, Fla.: Florida Department of Natural Resources.

CHAPTER FOURTEEN.   SWAMPED BY SEWAGE

Bay Institute of San Francisco. 1986. Selenium and agricultural drainage: Implications for San Francisco Bay and the California environment. Proceedings of the Second Selenium Symposium. Tiburon, Calif.

Cabelli, V. J., A. P. Defour, L. J. McCabe, and M. A. Levin. 1983. A marine recreational water quality criterion consistent with indicator concepts and risk analysis. *Journal of the Water Pollution Control Federation* 55:1306–14.

California Regional Water Quality Control Board. 1980. San Jose/Santa Clara Water Pollution Control Plant, August 1979 spill. Staff Report, Wil Brehns, Engineer, Oakland, Calif.

California State Water Resources Control Board. 1990. In the matter of the petition of Citizens for a Better Environment et al and City of San Jose. Order No. WQ 90-5. Sacramento, Calif.

———. 1990. *California municipal wastewater reclamation in 1987.* Office of Water Recycling, Sacramento, Calif.

Capuzzo, Judith, Anne McElroy, and Gordon Wallace. 1987. *Fish and Shellfish Contamination in New England Waters.* Report prepared for Coast Alliance, Washington, D.C.

Chesapeake Executive Council. 1985. *Chesapeake Bay Restoration and Protection Plan.* Annapolis.

Citizens for a Better Environment. 1990. *Hidden Polluters of California's Coast.* Report No. 90-2. San Francisco.

Congressional Budget Office. 1985. *Environmental Regulation and Economic Efficiency.* Washington, D.C.

Dynamac Corporation. 1989. *Use Impairments and Ecosystem Impacts of the New York Bight.* Rockville, Md.

Environmental Protection Agency. 1989. *Effectiveness of the Innovative and Alternative Wastewater Treatment Technology Program.* Report to Congress. Washington, D.C.

———. 1989. *Short-Term Action Plan for Addressing Floatable Debris in the New York Bight.* Washington, D.C.

———. 1990. *America's Sea at Risk.* First progress report on the Gulf of Mexico Program. Prepared for Gulf of Mexico Program, Stennis Space Center, Mich.

Heritage, John, ed. 1990. Saving the nation's great water bodies. *EPA Journal* 16(6).

Interstate Sanitation Commission. 1988. *Combined Sewer Outfalls in the Interstate Sanitation District.* New York, N.Y.

Marx, Wesley. 1971. *Man and His Environment: Waste.* New York: Harper & Row.

———. 1971. The fall and rise of sewage salvage. *Bulletin of Atomic Scientists* May.

National Oceanic and Atmospheric Administration. 1987. *Boston Harbor and Massachusetts Bay.* Estuarine Programs Office, Washington, D.C.

———. 1987. *Narragansett Bay.* Estuarine Programs Office, Washington, D.C.

———. 1987. *San Francisco Bay.* Estuarine Programs Office, Washington, D.C.

―――. 1988. *Hudson/Raritan Estuary.* Estuarine Programs Office, Washington, D.C.

―――. 1988. *The Quality of Shellfish Growing Waters in the Gulf of Mexico.* Report prepared by Dorothy Leonard and Marlene Broutman, Oceans Assessment Division, Rockville, Md.

―――. 1990. *The Quality of Shellfish Growing Waters on the West Coast of the United States.* Report prepared by Dorothy Leonard and Eric Slaughter, Oceans Assessment Division, Rockville, Md.

National Research Council. 1990. *Managing Troubled Waters.* Washington, D.C.: National Academy Press.

―――. 1990. *Monitoring Southern California's Coastal Waters.* Washington, D.C.: National Academy Press.

Natural Resources Defense Council. 1990. *The Poison Runoff Index for Greater Los Angeles.* Los Angeles.

New York Public Interest Research Group. 1988. *Wasted Water.* A citizen guide to sewage treatment plants in New York City. Prepared by Walter Liong-Ting Hang and Russ Haven. New York, N.Y.

Office of Technology Assessment. 1987. *Wastes in the Marine Environment.* Washington, D.C.

―――. 1990. *Finding the RX for Managing Medical Wastes.* Washington, D.C.

Puget Sound Water Quality Authority. 1991. *Puget Sound Water Quality Management Plan.* Lacey, Wash.

Save the Bay. *Annual Reports.* Providence, R.I.

Southern California Association of Governments. 1988. *The State of Santa Monica Bay.* Parts 1 and 2. Los Angeles.

**CHAPTER FIFTEEN.   THE SEAWARD MIGRATION OF POL-
LUTION**

Carr, Archie. 1986. Rips, FADS, and little loggerheads. *BioScience* 36(2).

Center for Environmental Conservation. 1987. *Plastics in the Ocean: More Than a Litter Problem.* Washington, D.C.

Center for Marine Conservation. 1990. *Cleaning North America's Beaches.* Washington, D.C.

Deans, Nora. 1989. Special issue on plastics in the oceans. *Current* 9(1).

General Accounting Office. 1988. *Degradable Plastics.* GAO/RCED-88-208. Washington, D.C.

Liebster, Jack. 1991. California's Adopt-A-Beach: More Than Just a Cleanup. San Francisco: California Coastal Commission.

MacKenzie, Debora. 1989. If you can't treat it, ship it. *New Scientist* April 1.

Mauro, Garry. 1987. Testimony before the U.S. Senate Committee on Commerce, Science and Transportation. July 29. Texas General Land Office, Austin, Tex.

National Park Service. 1989. *Marine Debris Survey.* Annual Report. Vegetation and Wildlife Division, Washington, D.C.

Texas General Land Office. 1987. *The Gulf of Mexico as a Special Area under MARPOL Annex V.* Report submitted to International Maritime Organization. Austin, Tex.

Weise, Bonnie, and William White. 1980. *Padre Island National Seashore.* Austin, Tex.: Bureau of Economic Geology, University of Texas.

EPILOGUE

Environmental Protection Agency. 1986. *Near Coastal Waters Strategic Options Paper.* Office of Marine and Estuarine Protection. Washington, D.C.

Office of Technology Assessment. 1987. *Wastes in the Marine Environment.* Washington, D.C.

United Nations Environment Program (UNEP). 1990. *State of the Marine Environment.* UNEP Regional Seas Reports and Studies No. 115. New York, N.Y.

National Research Council. 1990. *Monitoring Southern California's Coastal Waters.* National Academy Press, Washington, D.C.

Index